Making Sense of Java

Making Sense of Java

A guide for managers and the rest of us

BRUCE SIMPSON
JOHN D. MITCHELL
BRIAN CHRISTESON
A. REHAN ZAIDI
JONATHAN M. LEVINE

MANNING
Greenwich
(74° w. long.)

For electronic browsing of this book, see:
http://www.browsebooks.com

The publisher offers discounts on this book when ordered in quantity.

For more information please contact:
Special Sales Department
Manning Publications Co.
3 Lewis Street
Greenwich, CT 06830
or
LEE@MANNING.COM
Fax: (203) 661-9018

 Copyright © 1996 by Manning Publications Co.
All rights reserved.
Design and typesetting: Syd Brown
Copy editor: Thomas Barker
Cover design: Fernando Bunster
Copy proofing: Margaret Marynowski
Acquisitions Editor: Len Dorfman

Library of Congress Cataloging-in-Publication Data
Simpson, Bruce (1954–), et. al.
    Making Sense of Java: a guide for managers and the rest of us
        p. cm.
    Includes bibliographical references and index.
    ISBN 1-884777-24-4 (softcover)
    1. Java (Computer program language) I. Title.
    QA76.73.J38S56 1996
    005.13'3—dc20   96-14126
                                     CIP

Printed in the United States of America
2 3 4 5 6 7 8 9 - CR - 98 97 96

Dedications

Bruce Simpson
To Dorothy and Ray, many thanks

John D. Mitchell
To Shannon

Brian Christeson
To Jack Conner, who may have had fears of many kinds, but never
expected to give rise to a computer-language grammarian

A. Rehan Zaidi
To my family and R. M.

Jonathan M. Levine
For Susan

Contents

CONTENTS

CONTENTS

Introduction

Java is one of the hottest new technologies in the computer world today. While it is sometimes difficult for us to contain our enthusiasm, we will try to cut through the hyperbole and provide a clear view of this mist-shrouded island.

What this Book isn't

This book does not describe how to write Java programs—although it will be of interest to programmers who have heard of Java but are not sure how it may figure into their futures.

What this Book is

The target audience for this book is anyone who has heard about Java and its potential but wants objective information instead of the exaggerated claims presently flying about. Decision makers, project managers, team leaders, analysts, and even those with little more than idle curiosity will all find something of value here.

What is Java? Where did it come from? Where is it going? Will it change the face of computer systems as we know them? This book addresses all these important questions, so as to give the reader an understanding of Java, its origins, objectives, strengths, weaknesses, and potential. It explores the technical elements of the language, but also discusses the commercial implications for users and implementers of Java-based systems, making it an especially useful primer for those as interested in the bottom line as they are in the technological implications.

About the Authors

The authors of *Making Sense of Java* reside in New Zealand, the United States, and Canada, and relied heavily on technology described herein as they exchanged drafts, graphics, and cries of anguish. No applets were injured in the making of this book.

Bruce Simpson is an author, speaker, software developer, and consultant specializing in communications, with 18 years of industry experience and 10 years as a published writer. His other books include *The Internet Plain and Simple* and *The Internet in Business—Profit or Loss,* and a forthcoming volume on multi-platform development in C++.

Subsisting on caffeine, sugar, and too little sleep, **John D. Mitchell** has been a consultant for most of the last nine years, and has developed PDA software in OO assembly language at Geoworks. He funds his Java addiction by writing compilers, Tcl/Tk, C++, and Java systems. He writes two regular columns for *JavaWorld* magazine, and is currently developing a Java compiler.

Long an independent designer and programmer, **Brian Christeson** has turned a willingness to look foolish into ten years of highly successful lecturing in six countries and at more than a hundred of the Forbes 400. Five years of enthusiasm for the OO paradigm have led him into low company: he and John are writing professional courses and books about Java.

A. Rehan Zaidi is an engineering student at the University of Waterloo, and an editor of Digital Espresso—an online weekly summary of information about Java.

Jonathan M. Levine is a Principal of Infoscape, Inc., where he is designing Java systems that enable enterprise-wide collaboration and real-time, interactive data access. He previously designed and implemented the award-winning interface of Lotus Approach. Jonathan's experience includes more than 10 years of cross-platform object-oriented design and development at IBM, Lotus Development, and Oracle.

1

History

 It is safe to say that never in the history of computing has a new language come from obscurity to a key position in the industry in so short a time. What is it about Java that has intrigued so many people so quickly? Why are they talking about Java and why do many of them hail it as "the language of the future"? Perhaps we should start with a brief look at the history of Java and the company that created it.

Java was developed at Sun Microsystems, one of the giants in the computer industry. Its revenues approached $6 billion in 1995 and have been growing at a rate of 15 to 20 percent in recent years. These figures are strong indicators that Sun understands the demands of its market and is developing and providing products which accurately match them. Java may prove to be further proof of Sun's corporate acumen.

Ever since its formation in 1982, Sun has realized the value of networking as a means to provide maximum computing power in the most flexible and efficient form. Sun's war cry, "The network is the computer," exemplifies its wholesale embrace of the network paradigm. The network model is the source of many of today's popular buzzwords. "Client-server," "distributed processing," and other powerful new design strategies are finally allowing us to tap the power of multiple computers to provide increasingly more effective systems at lower prices.

Sun: "The network is the computer"

1

These new methodologies are not without their problems, however, and the limitations of traditional computer programming languages have proven in many ways to be their Achilles' heel.

Sun's answer to these problems is not only a new language but a new implementation paradigm, which, with an elegance and simplicity that belie its real power, solves many of the problems besetting adopters of these new technologies.

Java was designed to control PDAs and other consumer electronics products

Originally known as Oak, a name later changed to avoid trademark conflicts, Java has been under development since 1991. Sun originally intended to use Oak to develop software that would control consumer-electronics products. Built in anticipation of a future demand for such a system, Oak was conceived as an elegant, clean language with strong object-oriented features and an ability to provide seamless operation on multiple platforms. Oak was developed so quickly that it was ready long before its target market of sophisticated remote controls and Personal Digital Assistants (PDAs) existed.

Sun found itself with a solution in need of a problem, a predicament that did not take long to resolve. Because Oak, by now renamed Java, required a minimum of implementation effort on each new platform, it represented an ideal solution to many of the problems encountered when developing software that would work in an environment of increasingly heterogeneous networks. The rapid growth of the Internet, and the World Wide Web in particular, demanded a new type of technology, one that would address such important issues as platform independence and security, objectives Java was already designed to achieve.

The HotJava browser was the first Java application

With these issues in mind, the Java team produced a Web browser initially called Web Runner. This program later became the HotJava browser, Sun's showcase Java product and the first truly useful application based on the Java technology.

HotJava broke new ground. Unlike Mosaic and Netscape Navigator, it was a dynamic browser. By embedding small Java applications ("applets") in Web pages to provide animation, interaction, and intelligence, it brought life to Web pages that had largely been staid collections of text and static images. Though the first of these were as trivial in content as Bell's "Mr. Watson, come here; I need you", they demonstrated that we can use simple, secure, and portable Internet-based means to reap enormous benefits from distributed-processing and client-server technologies.

Sun announced Java and HotJava at the SunWorld conference in San Francisco in May 1995—and Netscape Communications announced at the same conference that its Navigator browser would support Java from late 1995 on. Almost at once many big names in the industry announced intentions to license the Java product and provide Java implementations and tools, thereby endorsing both the language and Sun's vision of the future.

Java went public in May 1995.

Overnight, the Internet began to buzz with animated talk about this exciting new product called Java. Thousands of developers and journalists crowded Sun's Web site to discover what the fuss was about. Sun wisely made pre-release versions of the Java Development Kit (JDK) available for download through the Internet. Soon developers all over the globe were exploring the potential of this new product.

Now, after a number of pre-release alpha and beta versions, release 1.0 of the JDK can be downloaded directly from Sun's Web site or any of several mirror sites. A handful of other commercial developers have also released 1.0 versions of their tools and libraries.

Why has Java enjoyed this meteoric rise to fame? In a word: timing. As with many revolutionary products, very few elements of Java are really new. Products have been demonstrating the potential of each of its underlying concepts in one form or another for many years. As long ago as the late 1970s, UCSD-P and other systems offered similar portability and hardware independence. Other systems have been long on distributed processing, security, or robustness. It is only now, though, that Java has put all the pieces together.

Java was the right product at the right moment

Fortunately for Sun, the growth of the Internet and the singular demands it places on software systems have coincided perfectly with the features and availability of Java. This "perfect fit," combined with the Internet's power to communicate new ideas effectively and distribute software easily, has created an unprecedented capability: never before have so many had such ready access to the resources needed to explore a product like Java.

Before Java's advent, C++ seemed to be Hobson's choice of language for the development of large-scale, performance-dependent applications. Now Java is being touted as the successor to C++, even as that language is supplanting C. Contrasting Java with C++ may give us a clearer idea why a language just out of its infancy receives such glowing endorsements.

Java may well replace C++ for large-scale software development

Many competent C programmers have found the transition to C++ slow and difficult. Not only must they come to grips with the radically different design and implementation methods inherent in the object-oriented paradigm, but they must also learn complicated new rules, grammar, and semantics. Implementations are inconsistent, and the continuing addition of features has made the very definition of the C++ language a rapidly moving target.

It becomes easy to see why many disappointed developers have failed to realize the enhanced productivity and reliability promised so enthusiastically by OO pundits. It is probably safe to say that many programmers are actually using C++ only as a slightly safer form of C, and avoiding many of the more advanced C++ features that could provide the benefits of an object-oriented approach.

Dismayed by the deficiencies and complexity of C++, many programmers have welcomed Java's power and simplicity. More than a few have described Java as "C++ the way it should have been done." It shares with C++ the concise, expressive nature of C-like syntax, but avoids enormous complications by abandoning backward compatibility, and by eliminating duplicate means of accomplishing the same objectives. It also adds multithreading, automatic garbage collection, and other features particularly useful in systems characterized by rapid, real-time interchange among many dissimilar processes executing simultaneously.

As is so often true of products designed and developed by a small team, the Java language is clean, consistent, and very elegant—features that can pay big dividends in reduced training costs, faster development cycles, improved productivity, enhanced system reliability, and reduced maintenance.

Because it breaks the present intimate dependence of applications on a particular operating system and processor, Java may even alter significantly the balance of power within the computer industry.

UNIX or OS/2? Windows or Mac? For years, the availability of particular software has influenced or even dictated the choice of an operating system, even a specific brand and model of computer—and vice versa. Temporary market advantages have spiraled into market dominance: if users can run the latest version of 1-2-3 today under Windows, but not until next year under OS/2, and not ever under Linux, which environment will they choose? If Lotus Development can sell 1-2-3 into a market of 40 million Windows users or 10 million OS/2 users, which version will it develop first?

Java could realign the industry as well as revolutionize programming

But what if adding a platform-independent language to the Internet and other technologies makes the elusive dream of interoperability among disparate systems a reality? When a software provider can create, not only a single source, but a single set of executable code that runs on any one of many platforms, what becomes of the massive dominance that industry giants like Microsoft and Intel currently enjoy in the microcomputer marketplace?

The smart money is on a Java-powered future

Trying to handicap winners and losers in the field of computing is usually the pastime of fools and gamblers. The nearly perfect match between Java's capabilities and the demands of today's marketplace, however, should make it an odds-on bet that the introduction of Java into the swelling stream of network-based and object-oriented technologies will be pivotal in determining the direction of the whole computer industry.

Both the developers and users of computing systems will find Java to be an important factor in their decision-making and marketing strategies. If indeed the network is the computer, then Java appears to be the single most effective tool for harnessing its full potential.

2

Where We Are,
How We Got There

 Before delving into the pros and cons of Java itself, we should assess the current state of an industry that seems to reinvent itself every decade. We can get some perspective on the importance of the Internet and of Java by looking briefly at how computer systems and computer programming languages have evolved over the last 30 years.

Interactive computer systems have evolved through four identifiable eras

Although it is difficult to draw a perfectly accurate time line for the evolution of computer systems, it is reasonable to talk about four eras: the monolith, the island, the bridge, and the world.

The Monolith: One Mainframe, Many Dumb Terminals

The first business computers processed "batches" of transactions and did not interact with end users at all. The first interactive systems were so large and expensive that they were cost-effective only for automating huge, time-sensitive tasks. These tasks tend to be distributed and organizational, such as processing clearinghouse transactions for banks, or booking and tracking airline reservations.

Large time-sharing mainframes dominated the monolithic era

A large, monolithic computer is often called a time-sharing system because it doles out the power of its large central processing unit (CPU) to its users in small segments of time. Users control and communicate with time-sharing systems via aptly named "dumb terminals:" simple, inexpensive computers that send and receive textual information to and from the central processor (see Figure 2.1).

Figure 2.1
Traditional multi-user computing

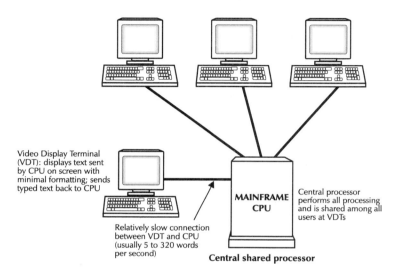

Video Display Terminal (VDT): displays text sent by CPU on screen with minimal formatting; sends typed text back to CPU

MAINFRAME CPU

Central processor performs all processing and is shared among all users at VDTs

Relatively slow connection between VDT and CPU (usually 5 to 320 words per second)

Central shared processor

The simplest dumb terminals, called Line Printing Terminals (LPTs) were little more than typewriters—printing the user's input and responses from the CPU on a long, continuous sheet of paper. Later terminals replaced the paper with a small, inexpensive video screen. Video-Display Terminals (VDTs) are much cheaper to operate and more convenient than their LPT predecessors. Although they superficially resemble today's personal computers, and some provide rudimentary formatting ability, they are really simply video typewriters: they can display only what their operators type in and what the CPU transmits to them.

Monolithic systems were relatively secure and easy to manage

Computing monoliths are very convenient for Information Systems (IS) administrators, because the "brain" of the system comes from a single manufacturer, and is completely contained in a central facility. Centralization and uniformity make these systems easy to expand, maintain, and secure.

CHAPTER 2 • WHERE WE ARE, HOW WE GOT THERE

When IS personnel see a need for more processing power, they can replace the components of the single, central CPU. When they maintain or enhance the system's software, users see the changes immediately at any terminal. Finally, compared to other systems, monoliths are very secure. Their instructions and data are all kept in a central place that can be locked and monitored around the clock, and communication between the computer and its users is traditionally by direct wire connection. Backups are made under a controlled regimen, and there is little risk of individuals stealing or sabotaging data.

Owners and users find monoliths to be awkward—for the same reasons their administrators find monoliths convenient.

Monolithic-era software was kinder to the hardware than to the users

VDTs are far less capable than personal computers. Most can display only 300 to 400 words at a time on a monochrome screen. This limitation often requires their operators to undergo extensive training to learn how to enter and interpret cryptic codes and displays. In addition, many monoliths communicate with users in block mode: they transmit information a full screen at a time rather than a character at a time. Between one screen and the next the computer cannot send new information to a user. Software for such systems is easier to develop than modern applications like word processors and database systems, but using it can be quite a challenge. When machines were expensive, this trade-off was a regrettable necessity, but now that processing power is cheap, overworking the user makes no sense.

Another disadvantage to monoliths is that both hardware and software are proprietary to their manufacturer. They may be easier to expand and maintain as a result, but such changes tend to be quite expensive. Monolith administration and programming require specialized expertise that is not germane to systems from other manufacturers. Changing vendors imposes huge costs, for new training as well as for new hardware and software. Even though software for

Their inflexibility has relegated monoliths to specialized, highly distributed tasks

monoliths is theoretically easy to update, end users usually cannot update these systems on their own. As a result, IS departments often find themselves backlogged with requests for updates and improvements.

For these reasons, monolithic computer systems are growing scarcer every year. They are still commonly used for very specialized and highly distributed tasks like airline reservations and sales of lottery tickets, and sometimes perform as very powerful file servers. Familiar monoliths include the IBM System/390, the CDC Cyber, and the Univac.

Minicomputers were cheaper, more flexible monoliths—with disadvantages of their own

Another option popular in the monolithic age was the minicomputer system. From the users' point of view, minicomputer systems are quite similar to mainframes: generally, users connect to them with standard dumb terminals or with specialized terminals like computerized cash registers or ATMs. Reduced purchase and enhancement costs make them attractive means to automate smaller tasks, such as record-keeping for a large retail store or one department of a corporation. Because most minicomputers do not communicate in block mode, they may be slightly easier to use than mainframes, but many are still limited by the capabilities of 80-column, 24-line terminals.

Minicomputers present more problems to IS departments than do mainframes. Maintaining scores of computers in far-flung locations poses new challenges. Nothing obliges a company to standardize on a single type of minicomputer, so finding administrators and programmers with the range of skills required to maintain and to write software for a heterogeneous population of minicomputers can be even harder than finding employees experienced in running a particular kind of mainframe.

Typical minicomputer systems are the Digital VAX, the IBM AS/400, and the Data General Aviion.

Distributed minicomputer systems provide welcome flexibility—at a price: When each department in a large organization has its own system, it can maintain, upgrade, and customize that system to its own changing needs, more cheaply and easily than if it were part of a monolithic system. Each department encounters obstacles, though, when it needs to share information with others that use different systems, especially if their computers are from different vendors.

Minicomputers shared data with difficulty, which led to networks of minis and mainframes

One way to overcome this problem is to connect an organization's individual minicomputers to a central mainframe, giving users at every location access to information from the other locations (see Figure 2.2). As in pure minicomputer systems, departments can expand an overloaded minicomputer more cheaply than a monolithic mainframe. Unlike pure mainframe or minicomputer systems, these hybrids facilitate information sharing via the central mainframe, without degrading the minicomputers' performance. Department-level IS staff can specialize in maintaining and customizing their local systems, making them more responsive; the central, corporate-level IS organization can concentrate on maintaining the central mainframe.

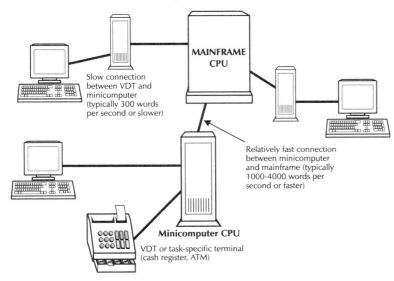

Slow connection between VDT and minicomputer (typically 300 words per second or slower)

MAINFRAME CPU

Relatively fast connection between minicomputer and mainframe (typically 1000-4000 words per second or faster)

Minicomputer CPU

VDT or task-specific terminal (cash register, ATM)

Figure 2.2
A mainframe/ minicomputer network

Minicomputer-mainframe networks can make computer systems cheaper for organizations to build and expand, but they are still difficult to learn and use, in part because they use the same dumb-terminal technology as pure mainframe and minicomputer systems. They also can be an order of magnitude harder to administer than more homogeneous systems. Sprawling networks of incompatible systems often cause huge headaches for corporate IS departments.

The Island: Personal Computers

Personal computers distributed significant processing power to individual users

For many readers, these discussions will seem like ancient history. Most of us are more familiar with Personal Computers (PCs) than with monolithic computers. Although they inherit most of their design concepts from large computers, as used in large organizations PCs are quite different from mainframe and minicomputer systems. Instead of hoarding processing power centrally, communities of PCs distribute it to individual users, who can take advantage of it at need rather than queue up for a share of a central resource.

As PCs have become more and more powerful, they have required less and less sophistication of their users. The power advantage that a PC has over a dumb terminal enables programmers to gear PC software for the novice. Attractive, intuitive displays and extensive online reference material replace the cryptic screens and codes of the mainframe world. Individual users determine PC capabilities for themselves, adding peripherals and software that meet their needs and wants.

PCs also let an organization "right-size" computing capacity—and costs. Instead of providing shared access to a single expensive, relatively inflexible system, an organization gives users inexpensive PCs with power and functionality appropriate to their needs.

PCs taken by themselves pose two major problems, however. First, they are islands. Where mainframe users share data easily, many PC users do so only with difficulty. They use incompatible programs and files with conflicting formats. Both shareware programmers and commercial houses have produced tools to address these problems, but their success has been mixed, and file conversion can never be as convenient as simple uniformity. Even a trivial matter like the storage limit of a floppy diskette may be a significant obstacle.

PCs' isolation made administration and data sharing difficult

Second, the flexibility that makes PCs so popular with users presents a huge problem for corporate IS departments. Deploying and upgrading PC software can be a nightmare for administrators. The ease with which users can tailor PCs to their tastes can make it difficult for administrators to diagnose problems of individual systems, and users complicate the problem by installing unapproved software. Even organizations that set and enforce standards requiring use of software from specific vendors find subtle differences between products produced at different times.

The Bridge: Local-Area Networks

To be fair, even our discussion of the island era is primarily historical. Just as the dumb terminal has largely become a relic, most modern organizations no longer have archipelagoes of isolated PCs. At home our PCs typically stand alone, but at the office we routinely hop from island to island over bridges created by local-area networks (LANs).

Local networks allowed PCs to share data—inefficiently

A typical local-area network is composed of several PCs, sometimes called workstations, connected to one or more file servers, sometimes simply called servers. The server may be another PC, a minicomputer, or a mainframe. In a classical file-server/workstation model (see Figure 2.3), each workstation is solely responsible for all the processing required to perform any given task. The server's primary role is to act as a shared hard disk. It provides safe, centralized access to shared information, peripherals, and mainframe gateways. A workstation interacts with the file server as it would with one of its own hard drives or peripherals, reading and writing every bit and byte of information via transmissions across the network.

Figure 2.3
A traditional PC-based local area network

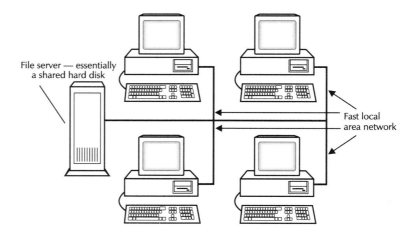

File server — essentially a shared hard disk

Fast local area network

Simple LANs are adequate for small numbers of PCs that transmit data sequentially...

This approach is adequate if the workstation-based programs read and write data infrequently and sequentially, as when a word processor loads or saves an entire document. The network can handle fairly large data transfers, so long as they do not require detailed interaction.

The bridge is a wonderful advance over the island for users. The LAN allows them all the flexibility of PCs, yet enables them to share information with ease. Further, it provides a starting point for genuine shared applications by enabling individual computers to communicate quickly and transparently. The LAN lightens at least one burden of PC administrators by storing shared information in a central place.

...but they add to administrators' burdens, and easily run into performance problems

Unfortunately, it replaces that burden with others: in addition to supporting applications, PC administrators must install and maintain network-client software on each user's system.

Worse yet, the simple file-server/workstation model breaks down when programs transfer ever larger amounts of data across the network. While a powerful server may have more than one CPU, only one computer on each LAN can "talk" at a time. A workstation-based program that searches for small pieces of data in large files interacts with the server in a flood of fragmentary requests and responses. When individual users place such heavy demands on a single shared network, they begin to overload it very quickly, and all users see performance deteriorate rapidly.

To see more precisely how this problem arises, we need only imagine supporting an airline reservation system with a traditional file-server/workstation LAN. To find a booking, a workstation will have to search the reservations file. Any particular reservation might be close to the file's beginning or to its end, but on average the workstation will need to read through half the file. To conduct its search, the workstation will ask the file server to start at the beginning of the file and then transmit every record until the workstation finds the correct one (see Figure 2.4). A typical network can transfer up to 150,000 words per second, but that will be nowhere near fast enough for an airline that makes, changes, and cancels hundreds of thousands of reservations a day. Airline agents would find such a system unusable.

An intensely interactive system quickly uncovers the limitations of a simple LAN

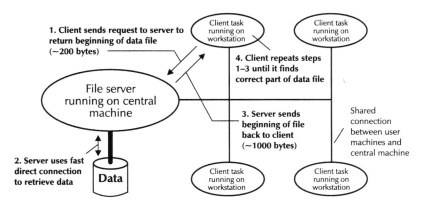

Figure 2.4
Searching a database on a file-server/workstation network. Workstation tasks perform search operations, overloading the server and the network.

Inevitable performance degradation renders this type of design unsuitable for large database systems. As an analogy to the file-server/workstation model, consider a self-serve supermarket. Users roam the store individually, collecting the items they want. Supermarkets are wonderfully convenient when they are not crowded, but at peak hours too many customers trying to collect too many items results in collisions, traffic jams, and long lines at the checkout stands.

The file-server/workstation model has a flaw similar to that of the mainframe monolith, but in reverse: it treats the central computer, the file server, as no more than a dumb hard drive.

We can improve performance of such systems by having workstations and file servers share the processing more effectively, and by packaging communications more intelligently. Distributing the workload among multiple computers avoids overloading any one of them; smart bundling of requests and responses reduces the total load on all processors, and on the network itself. Both improve overall system performance, yet neither forces us to upgrade or overhaul large components of the system.

We call these more intelligent LANs "client-server" systems. The "client" is the application running on the workstation that requests services; the "server" is the software on the central computer that fills the requests. In a contrast to our supermarket analogy, we can picture a client-server system as a streamlined version of the old-fashioned general store.

In bygone days, a customer requested a list of products from a clerk behind the counter, and the clerk responded by locating the desired goods and bringing them directly to the customer. Because clerks knew how to work around each other, and knew exactly where everything was kept, they could fill orders quickly and efficiently. The best clerks could fill several orders in a single trip around the shop's shelves, achieving even greater efficiency.

The general store faded away as rising wages made the use of human servers increasingly uneconomical. In the world of computer systems, however, server costs have been dropping steadily for years. They have reached a level at which a new form of the general-store model provides a cost-effective solution to problems we have identified.

The "general store model" is reborn in a new environment

A typical client-server system features many "virtual store clerks" working in a carefully coordinated manner that avoids collisions or conflicts, and serving a large number of "customers" simultaneously, with minimal delays. Like the most efficient of their predecessors, these virtual clerks bundle several requests at a time to improve performance still further.

The client-server database is among the most common systems of this kind (see Figure 2.5). A database server and workstations communicate in a set of well-defined, concise, high-level instructions. When a client workstation needs one or more records from a central file, it sends a single request containing relevant search criteria to the server, which then places the request in a queue. The server task processes each request in turn; using its fast, direct connection to the database, it locates and returns all of the records that match the criteria.

A client-server database distributes tasks appropriately, and communicates efficiently

Because the client issues a single compact request instead of a long series of small interactions, and because the server returns only the data specifically requested, the load on the network diminishes dramatically. When communications occur only in short bursts, the network can serve a larger number of clients more responsively.

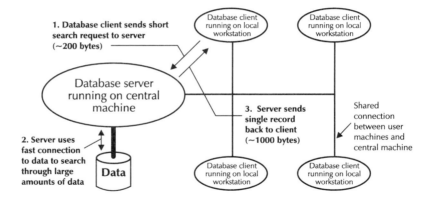

Figure 2.5
Searching a database on a client-server network
**Database server performs all search operations, reducing the workload on
the network and the workstations.**

*Even client-server LANs
suffer problems of
compatibility and scope*

Even the more intelligent LANs share some of the limitations
common to minicomputer systems: because LANs often
spring up department by department, many organizations
end up with a plethora of incompatible networks, and users
on different LANs cannot easily share information.

Some network software is hard to administer, and installing
or upgrading applications distributed across many servers
and client machines can be a major undertaking.

We cannot solve these problems by connecting everyone to a
single large LAN. Electrical limitations, reliability problems,
and the difficulty of sharing a single resource among many
users limit LANs to small, local groups. Physical constraints
limit the length of a LAN connection to a few hundred
yards—adequate for offices, but not for networks that may
span continents. Moreover, a typical LAN connects all computers to a single cable, and any damage to that cable affects
everyone on the network.

This single-wire design has another flaw: like an old-fashioned telephone "party line," it prevents more than two
computers from communicating at the same time. Hundreds
of "calls" are made and disconnected each second, so a
single cable is adequate for small groups. The more comput-

ers we add to the LAN, however, the harder it becomes for any two of them to communicate at any particular time. The strain grows exponentially as the number of computers on the network increases.

The World: Wide-Area Networks

To provide the features of the LAN to all of their users, many organizations have implemented wide-area networks (WANs). Wide-area networks use specialized computers called routers to manage communications among LANs. A router keeps track of all the computers connected to a LAN, and examines all the data moving across that LAN. If a packet of data is part of a conversation between two computers on the same LAN, the router ignores it. If it is part of a conversation between a local computer and one on another LAN, the router transmits the data to another router closer to the other LAN.

Networks of networks allow enterprise-wide data sharing

To the user, the wide-area network resembles a company-wide LAN. In breadth of scope, it closely resembles a minicomputer-mainframe network; the biggest difference is that it features smart systems at all points in the network, including the workstations. Users throughout the organization have access to the data they need, and to extremely powerful applications.

Of course, while the WAN may solve an organization's connectivity problems, it magnifies many of the administrative difficulties that characterize LANs. Software deployment is an even bigger headache, and a network that comprises hundreds, or thousands, or tens of thousands of computers will almost certainly include dozens of types—a nightmare for programmers and administrators.

Administrative problems increase with network size

The Internet: The Global WAN

We can picture the Internet as many things, but in implementation it is simply a single, very large WAN. Its

*The Internet extends
WAN capabilities—and
problems—to the world*

advantages and disadvantages are similar to those of a corporate WAN (sometimes called an "intranet" or "corporate net"), only magnified. It allows users in different organizations to share data and applications; because it is decentralized, damage to one part of the Internet does not affect others, and it is ubiquitous.

Of course, the Internet comprises a mind-boggling variety of computers. The sheer range of this diversity tends to exacerbate the incompatibility problems among individual machines, and it makes traditional deployment practically impossible. Netscape Navigator is probably the only client-server application that has been installed on nearly every computer on the Internet.

Another problem area is, in its scope at least, unique to the Internet: security. A corporate WAN is at least local to a single enterprise, is physically disconnected from the rest of the world, and is the property of a single owner. These constraints do not guarantee security, by any means, but they do make problems more manageable. By contrast, the Internet is global, open-ended, unowned—and easily compromised.

Because the Internet consists of a vast array of independent yet interconnected computers, data sent across the Internet may pass through many different machines before it reaches its destination (see Figure 2.6). Each stop along the way presents opportunities for interception and eavesdropping. In the early days of the Internet little of the information carried was commercially sensitive, but today organizations conduct an increasing amount of business over the Internet, posing problems that demand an entirely new set of solutions.

*Who sent it?
Who received it?
How can we know?*

The prospect of dispatching a message containing sensitive material through the 'net raises a chilling question: Who will be listening? Another question can arise when reading a message: Who is doing the talking? The Internet itself provides no inherent way to guarantee a truthful answer to either question.

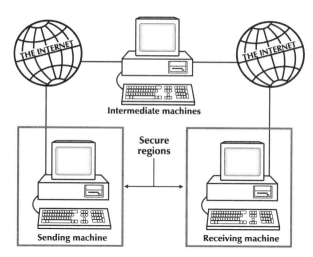

Figure 2.6
Typical communication via the Internet

Users have begun to use software to enhance communications security. For example, the security-conscious use encryption to protect a message's contents and authentication to verify its sender's identity with a "digital signature." Security software typically relies on paired programs running at each end of the transmission (see Figure 2.7). A typical example is PGP (Pretty Good Privacy), which offers a high level of protection, but requires both sender and recipient to perform a separate explicit operation.

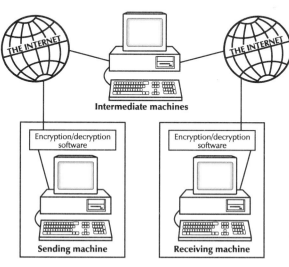

Figure 2.7
Secure Internet communication, using encryption and decryption.

Some software companies have built security features into their communications products, eliminating the need for separate encryption and decryption steps. In addition, some hardware companies are working on systems that build this kind of security into routers, creating the potential for transparent encryption among local-area networks that use the Internet as their WAN. We will discuss security concerns in more detail in Chapter 8.

Processor + Operating System = Platform

Complications are the price we pay for functionality

The diversity of existing systems has exacerbated nearly every problem we have described. Many large organizations seem to have at least one of every popular "platform" (for our purposes, defined as the combination of a processor and an operating system). Even machines that look identical may be different platforms; for example, Pentium-driven IBM PCs support Windows NT, OS/2, Linux, Novell Netware, and many other operating systems. This variety allows individuals to customize their tools to their jobs, but it requires the creation, purchase, and use of many different versions of the same products.

If we start to daydream about the appeal of standardizing on a single system design, the words of Henry Ford advertising his Model T bring us back to earth: "You can have any color you want as long as it's black." And a comparison of a Model T's 35-mph top speed and less-than-plush upholstery with the performance and comfort of today's automobiles should be convincing evidence of the benefits of competition.

To remain competitive, every manufacturer in our own industry strives to produce a system that is the fastest, most versatile, powerful, and cost-effective for a particular set of tasks. The result is a variety of systems that are increasingly capable—and incompatible, in at least two dimensions: processors and operating systems.

The heart of every computer is its processor, the component responsible for executing the individual instructions that make up a program. Each manufacturer has its own notions of what represents the ideal set of instructions a system should support. More often than not, variations result in total incompatibility among processors. A single program will not run on both an IBM mainframe and an Apple Macintosh because their instruction sets are so different.

Processor variations oblige developers to support multiple versions of their software...

The traditional solution to the processor compatibility problem has been to write software in a portable high-level language such as BASIC or C++, and let a compiler translate the high-level language to the machine language of each desired processor. This strategy has worked well for companies like Oracle. Some computer manufacturers and software companies try to support legacy code with emulation software or other mechanisms, with considerable success: Intel has produced a half dozen generations of chips that remain compatible with the 8088 of the original IBM PC, and Apple successfully managed its transition from the 68000 to the PowerPC.

Differences among operating systems, the software that "runs closest to the machine," can pose even larger problems for programmers, even when processors are identical. For example, IBM's OS/2 and Microsoft's Windows run on the same kinds of computers but manage processor, memory, and peripherals very differently; programs written for OS/2 will not run under Windows 95.

...and so do operating-system differences

Like manufacturers of processors, operating-system vendors attempt to support legacy code; for example, both OS/2 and Windows 95 run MS-DOS and Windows 3.1 software. Other companies provide software "tool kits" to ease "porting" of programs from one operating system to another.

Modern operating systems are so complex, however, that few porting projects are thoroughly successful. Even a tool kit's help usually does not preclude considerable recoding, which makes many such endeavors uneconomical.

The variety of platforms causes software development costs to explode

Even when it is feasible to create versions of a software product for multiple platforms, programmers then face the daunting task of keeping them up to date. Maintenance costs increase exponentially with the number of versions supported; sustained development on a cross-platform project is often many times more expensive than on a single-platform project.

The Need for a New Paradigm

A vastly broader user base increases demands on software in two directions

As computers become as common as stereos, telephones, and televisions, the average sophistication of users diminishes. The emergence of the networked computer as a household appliance will oblige both hardware and software developers to make connecting computers as easy as plugging in telephones, and software installation as easy as inserting video tapes.

At the same time users require simplicity of operation, they also demand more and more functionality. Software developers face the task of creating ever larger, ever more sophisticated products in shorter periods of time. The Internet boom seems to be adding yet another layer of complexity, all but forcing applications to offer client-server capability.

Incremental advances will not be enough; we need an entirely new way to produce software

Alas, as the power of our computers and complexity of our applications grow at exponential rates, many software developers are discovering that advances in tools and techniques do not keep pace with the demands placed upon them. Customers complain about the quality of commercial software; developers complain about the complexity and fragility of existing code bases. As it has in the past, the industry must transform the way it develops software.

3

Where Do We Go From Here?

 The complexity of modern computer systems seems to increase daily. Users and programmers seem bewildered, and barely able to muddle through their work. In areas outside computing, however, we can find many examples of complex, distributed technologies that appear simple to their consumers and their integrators. For example, the global telephone network is made up of billions of feet of wire, hundreds of millions of telephones, and countless switches, operators, and designers. While this system is indeed complex and distributed, it is easy to install a telephone, a fax machine, or even a video conferencing system, and even easier to use a telephone. What makes such systems more approachable than most software systems?

The individual pieces of equipment that make up the telephone system appear simple because the implementation details of each device are encapsulated, or hidden, from every other part. We do not need to know how a fax machine works to install it, only the kind of cable needed to connect it to our phone system. In fact, a hardware designer doesn't have to know how the telephone system works in order to build a fax machine—to build a device that will operate correctly on the telephone network, only a very limited set of facts is needed.

Hardware systems use encapsulation to reduce complexity

Encapsulation in the telephone system is so complete that few noticed when the transmission of calls was gradually upgraded from analog to digital over the last twenty years. The changeover was transparent because the specific methods of transmission are encapsulated in the switching system.

Computers in networks cooperate much as do people in large organizations

One might argue that computers are more general-purpose and more complex than telephones, but there are many examples of people working in large networks to solve extremely complex problems. In fact, there are many parallels between computer networks and the behavior of persons in large organizations.

One can think of PCs in the global network as individual workers, of LANs as work groups or departments, of file servers as expert consultants and librarians, of administrators and programmers as managers and directors, and of routers and WANs as the organizational infrastructure that keeps the business running. Just as in a large and dispersed human organization, maximizing the power of a computer network requires a division of labor among members. Such a division of labor can be surprisingly powerful: recently, a small group of researchers was given a coded message and was told that its author estimated it would take eons to decipher; using a computer network they broke the code in a matter of months.

Coworkers and computers divide tasks, use a common vocabulary, and balance workloads

Successful division of labor does not require that all people work alike. It does require, however, that they have a way to break down large tasks into smaller parts, a way to communicate tasks to members that includes a common vocabulary, and a way to "load balance"—to enable team members who finish their tasks to pitch in and help other team members.

These principles for division of labor work for computer systems as well as for human systems. Hardware manufacturers have been moving toward interoperability by modularizing and standardizing their products. They have replaced the spaghetti-like wiring of early computers with self-contained modules of many sizes: chips, circuit boards, subassemblies, devices, and so on ("breaking down large tasks into smaller parts"). They have also reduced a potentially bewildering variety of possible connectors to a limited set of relatively simple plugs and jacks (the "common vocabulary"). Sophisticated processors divide tasks among units at lower levels in a way that uses them up to their capacity ("load balancing").

We could well reason that similar strategies would help us cut the complexity of computer software used across heterogeneous networks.

How do Java and the simple concepts behind it address these issues? Java provides an easy way for programmers to make use of some important developments from research in computer science: portability and platform independence, object-oriented programming, distributed program code, and distributed processing. As we will discover in this chapter, application of these ideas enables software designers to distribute tasks in much the same way managers in large organizations distribute work.

Can software systems use the same strategies to reduce their complexity?

Breaking Tasks into Smaller Parts: Object-Oriented Programming

At the heart of each computer is its central processing unit (CPU), which manipulates data in relatively small amounts and with relatively simple instructions. As recently as twenty years ago, it was common to develop even large software systems in low-level "assembly language," simple human-readable instructions that translated directly to corresponding machine instructions. Some very large and impressive systems have been written in assembly language, including the software for the space missions, as well as many early commercial software products.

Software written in assembly language can be extremely efficient—and efficiency was essential when computing power was very expensive. Unfortunately, assembly language requires programmers to write every single instruction their computer will execute, and to take into account the characteristics that set it apart from other computers, in detail—very time-consuming. Language that uses the machine efficiently thus tends to use programmers inefficiently.

Programming consists of translating problem solutions expressed in abstract, human terms ("Print an invoice") into concrete instructions simple enough for the computer to understand (equivalent to "Fetch the current invoice total from over there; fetch the item amount from over here; increase the first amount by the second..."). If programmers must worry constantly about the minutiae of storing, retrieving, and processing information, it is very difficult for them to keep their original objectives in mind.

Structured Programming

Structured programming, a widely used design methodology, has helped programmers maintain their focus for many years. It encourages them to map out the abstractions first, in multiple layers, then proceed to write the detailed instructions only in small, discrete, easily managed chunks.

As more advanced computer languages came along, they eased the burden on programmers. "High-level languages" provide sets of instructions which are more distant from the machine. A single high-level instruction bundles a long series of machine instructions into a compact form programmers can more easily understand and manipulate. Programmers can then collect series of high-level instructions into even larger, still more abstract instructions. Software tools called compilers later reverse this process, breaking the programmer's abstract representation of the program down into the detailed instructions the machine can execute.

This process of starting with a set of instructions provided to us, then encapsulating larger and larger parts of a complex program, parallels the way we use human languages, in which we start with a received vocabulary, then collect words into phrases, phrases into sentences, and so on to express complex ideas.

High-level programming introduced one kind of encapsulation

High-level languages like C, Pascal, and FORTRAN facilitate the process of programming in a structured way. By lightening the programmer's load, high-level programming results in more reliable code in less time than with assembly-language programming—although the code will execute more slowly. As processors have become cheaper and faster, and compilers more sophisticated, raw execution speed has become less important than development speed. Software companies succeed by writing and revising programs more quickly, not by writing quicker programs. The more successfully a high-level language allows programmers to encapsulate, the more productive they can be.

Object Orientation and Encapsulation

As software has grown ever more complex, however, even the structured programming model is proving inadequate to the demands that today's software projects make on it. Traditional languages like Pascal and C facilitate structured programming at the level of a single program, but do little to ensure the reliable development of large projects by teams of programmers. This limitation is the main reason many organizations are considering or have already moved to object-oriented programming. Managing large projects is much easier when features of the language support team-oriented design and construction.

The structured paradigm is inadequate for the much larger systems of today

One major problem with structured programming is the separation of data from algorithm. Traditional languages let programmers collect small pieces of related information together into abstractions (often confusingly) called structures, but they make the data and the instructions that manipulate them separate parts of the program.

In a traditional system, an invoice is only a collection of data

For example, take the case of a program designed to perform certain operations on an invoice. Within the computer's memory, the information contained within an actual invoice is stored in a data area whose structure has been defined by a programmer (see Figure 3.1). In this example, a programmer has given each piece of data on the invoice form its own storage area within the Invoice structure, giving code anywhere in the program access to the data by name.

Figure 3.1
A real-world invoice and its representation in a data structure

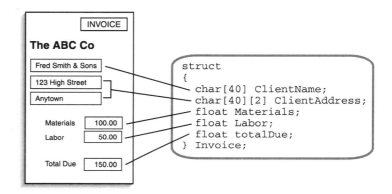

In a traditional structured program, the Invoice structure is simply a template for data. In order to get or modify an Invoice, a programmer must have direct access to its individual data components. Each component might be accessed from many different parts of the program (see Figure 3.2). Defining data in one part of the program and manipulating them in another often leads to software defects. Such defects multiply if the Invoice structure is changed after initial development is complete. Changing the structure obliges maintenance staff to find every line of code affected by the change, and it is all too easy to miss one. That one line can later change Invoice data in some subtly incorrect way, creating a bug that may be very hard to find and fix.

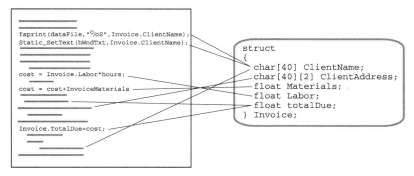

```
fsprint(dataFile,"%oS",Invoice.ClientName);
Static_SetText(hWndTxt,Invoice.ClientName);


cost = Invoice.Labor*hours;
cost = cost+InvoiceMaterials



Invoice.TotalDue=cost;
```

```
struct
{
    char[40] ClientName;
    char[40][2] ClientAddress;
    float Materials;
    float Labor;
    float totalDue;
} Invoice;
```

Figure 3.2
A data structure manipulated by many parts of a program

Programmers often need to define data structures that differ from each other only in part: a Service Invoice may include some components that are unique, and some that it shares with a Product Invoice. Traditional programming languages do not provide easy means to represent these similarities and differences. In C, for instance, a programmer must create a separate data definition and a separate set of code for each distinct invoice type. Not only is this a waste of time, space, and energy, but it also magnifies the potential for bugs to creep into the software. In order to synchronize changes made to data definitions that are similar but not identical, programmers must often examine and change large amounts of code.

Conventional languages make it hard to manage subtle variations in data types

The hardware world uses encapsulation to avoid many of these problems. For example, when a computer wants to access data on a hard drive, it sends a generic command to the hard drive to fetch the data, and the hard drive returns the data in a generic and predefined way. As long as the computer asks for the data correctly, and the hard drive returns the data correctly, any hard drive can be used with any computer.

Can software accomplish this kind of encapsulation? Advocates of the object-oriented (OO) paradigm claim it can. An Object-Oriented Programming System (OOPS) provides support for abstraction of kinds impossible in the structured model. A well designed OO system can provide complex

Object orientation takes the practice of encapsulation to a new level

functionality with code that is smaller and better organized. Programmers can produce more reliable systems more quickly and maintain them more easily.

OO programming builds on structured programming, but adds entirely new concepts, among them "object" and "class." These terms are too often used interchangeably. Properly speaking, an object is one actual thing, such as the Invoice our program is printing right now. A class is a category of things; the Invoice being printed now is only one instance of the Invoice class. If an Invoice were no more than a data structure, we would say that its data definition is a class definition, and the block of data needed to bill a particular customer for a particular service constitutes an Invoice object. Classes are not just data definitions, however, and objects are much more than the data they contain.

Objects encapsulate both code and the data it manipulates

Structured programming encouraged us to encapsulate small pieces of code inside larger ones, but relegated data to another area of the program. Class definitions allow programmers to bundle not only data components, but the code that operates on them. Each object acts as if each operation defined by the class is as much a part of itself as the specific data it contains. An Invoice object is not just information: it is functionality as well.

An OO program is not a collection of instructions operating at a distance on a collection of data; it is a collection of self-contained objects interacting with each other. Each is responsible for all operations on its own data, and no other object has direct access to its components.

This "data hiding" makes objects much more like components of hardware systems, with the same potential for reliability. When we find it necessary to modify the data pattern of a class of objects, we know exactly where to find every line of code that might be affected by our change— right there, in the same class. We replace the tedious and error-prone task of finding and fixing lines of code scat-

CHAPTER 3 • WHERE DO WE GO FROM HERE?

tered across a large system with the much more manageable task of making careful changes within a narrow and clearly defined scope.

Returning to the Invoice example, suppose we define an Invoice *class* instead of an Invoice *structure* (see Figure 3.3). We define both the data components each Invoice must contain *and* all the operations that use them. At run time, each Invoice object is a "black box." Other objects cannot peek at the values stored inside or change them. If an object needs, for example, the Invoice's total, it requests that information from the Invoice object. If it needs to change billing terms, it issues a different request to the Invoice.

As an object, an invoice can include code that reports values and allows updates

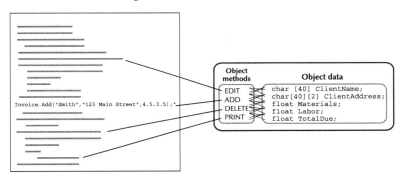

Figure 3.3
An object providing services to many parts of a program

Encapsulating data and instructions in this way simplifies the interface between the Invoice and other objects in the program, and reduces the chance of programmer error by reducing inadvertent side effects. Once the Invoice class has been created, tested, and debugged, even the programmer that created it is no longer concerned about its internal workings. All that is needed is a list of its operations and an understanding of how they are requested.

Object Orientation and Inheritance

In addition to vastly improved encapsulation, OO systems provide a mechanism to extend the behavior of a class, called inheritance. To see how inheritance works, we can return to the Invoice example.

OO also helps us manage data variants—and reuse existing code in the bargain

Suppose a programmer has created the Invoice class above, and two other programmers want to create specialized types of invoices (see Figure 3.4). Instead of duplicating the functionality of the basic Invoice class in each variant, they simply inherit all its data and code. They are then free to specialize their variants in different ways, each adding new components, new operations, or both. No new code is needed to take advantage of inherited operations that work as well for the variant as for the original class; if any need tailoring the programmer can override them with new operations.

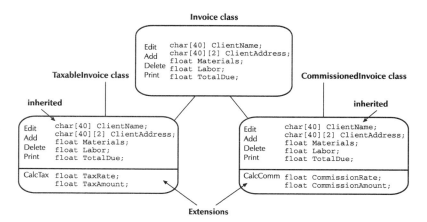

Figure 3.4
Creating new classes by inheriting from one existing class—single inheritance

Developers have long found it difficult to reuse code above a low level of abstraction. By inheriting the code of existing classes, developers can now achieve reuse at levels once inconceivable to them, and increase their productivity tenfold. Centralizing the development of common operations in a single class frees the programmers of our two variants to concentrate on specializing them. They gain leverage not only from the first class programmer's development effort, but from subsequent maintenance as well: changes made to the original Invoice class are automatically reflected in the variants.

Figure 3.4 illustrates a simple form of inheritance, usually called single inheritance. Some object-oriented systems also support a more complex form, multiple inheritance, which allows a new class to inherit the attributes of more than one existing class (see Figure 3.5).

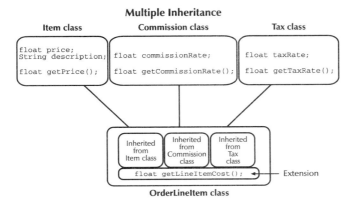

Figure 3.5
Creating a new class by inheriting from more than one class—multiple inheritance

There is still some controversy about the use of multiple inheritance in object-oriented systems. When used judiciously, it can simplify the design and construction of complex systems by allowing a broader structuring of classes and more extensive code reuse. However, by including not just operation names but also data and operation implementations, multiple inheritance can add an exponential degree of complexity to programs, and so many OOPS practitioners eschew it.

Multiple inheritance and interfaces provide two different ways to skin a very tough cat

Instead, some languages (including Java) rely on "interfaces," which appear similar to classes but have no implementation. When defining a new class, a programmer can specify one or more interfaces that it will implement. From the outside, the new class exhibits the behavior of all the specified interfaces, much as if they were classes and it had inherited from them. This tactic may not seem as straightforward at first, but it accomplishes similar objectives with fewer complications.

Taken together, encapsulation and inheritance give OO programmers the ability to construct software systems from self-contained objects, which can both hold data and ma-

OO revolutionizes the way we organize software

nipulate it. They can create libraries of classes which can be reused in new projects the same way basic electronic components can be rearranged to build new hardware. Developers can use classes to build programs the way that children use Lego blocks to build toys—simply clicking them together to create new systems instead of redeveloping the same blocks over and over again. Our invoice classes can be adapted for use in a wide range of applications either directly, by creating instances of them, or through inheritance, by adding new data fields and new or modified operations.

Realizing the Potential of Object Orientation

Why have we not yet seen gains in productivity that were promised?

While OOPS promises to improve significantly the productivity and reliability of large software projects, very few organizations have realized its potential by using the most popular OO language, C++. The reasons are manifold, and frequently the subject of hot debate within the industry.

Language complexity?

Some blame the language's complexity and inconsistencies, citing the productivity of programmers using pure object-oriented languages like Eiffel and Smalltalk. With its size and complexity, C++ threatens to become another Ada or PL/1, a language so big and complex that programmers tend to restrict themselves to their own chosen subset. This problem is exacerbated by continuing revision of the C++ language specification. Over its short life many new features have been added to overcome shortcomings in its original design. These revisions not only compromise the effectiveness of the language as a development tool, they can also cause significant problems in the area of program maintenance.

Inadequate training?

Others blame the "failure" of OOPS on inadequate training, claiming that too many programmers make the transition from C to C++ without fully understanding the OO paradigm. Since C++ shares most of the syntax and semantics of C, many C programmers begin using C++ without any formal training in the concepts or practical implementation of object-oriented techniques. This backward compatibility is what made C++ a marketplace success initially: its ability to capitalize on the existing base of C code and the knowledge of C programmers. Unfortunately, this compatibility has also hindered realization of its full potential as an object-oriented language.

Retraining is a capital-intensive investment with a relatively protracted pay-back term, and the pressure of delivery deadlines and limited budgets often pushes training into the background in favor of simply getting systems to the market. The result is a large number of programmers who understand the basic syntax and semantics of C++ but simply use it as another structured programming language, in effect treating it as little more than new version of C. Their organizations, while paying lip-service to OO, never actually achieve the benefits of object-oriented programming.

This pattern has its precedents. When structured programming was first finding acceptance, many organizations resisted the transition from assembly language to high-level languages. They claimed they could use structured techniques to implement their software in an essentially unstructured manner. The theory may have been sound, but they often found they could not force their development staffs to use structured programming techniques. Given old habits and the reality of deadlines, many programmers ignored them in favor of expediency.

Inertia?

By contrast, organizations that moved their teams to true structured languages like Pascal found that the languages enforced modularity and structured programming on the developers. The end result for these organizations was that, after a short learning curve, teams produced more software more reliably in a shorter period of time.

Object-oriented languages like Smalltalk and Java can do for structured programmers what Pascal and C did for assembly-language programmers: force them to rethink their strategies, to learn a new paradigm in order to use the new language. The lack of structured constructs like functions and structures, and the presence of object-oriented constructs such as methods and classes, force programmers to learn and use object-oriented techniques. For example, they cannot create any Java program without defining and instantiating at least one class. The result will likely be that, again after a learning curve, development teams produce even more software even more reliably and even more quickly.

Is Java the solution?

Of course, once an organization has chosen to move to object-oriented programming, a big decision remains: which language to choose. Sun's Java white paper claims that Java incorporates the best parts of mainstream object-oriented languages like Smalltalk, Objective-C, and C++, but avoids the complexity of C++. Some proponents of the other languages disagree with this claim, saying that Java doesn't go far enough in supporting the OO paradigm. For example, some C++ programmers argue that it was unreasonable to leave out mechanisms they consider extremely useful in the effective implementation of object-oriented software, such as multiple inheritance and operator overloading.

Java does provide the basic mechanisms necessary for the implemention of object-oriented systems. In addition, it implements powerful object-oriented techniques not available in C++, which make it practical to update existing programs via relatively slow media like telephone lines.

A Common Vocabulary: Portability and Platform Independence

As we discussed in Chapter 2, most existing development systems are designed to produce executable code that is specific to a particular processor and operating environment. The production of this platform-specific code means that software compiled for one model of computer, such as the Apple Macintosh, will not run on another model, such as an

IBM-compatible PC. Making the same program work on more than one platform requires that its source code be translated, or ported, to each platform (see Figure 3.6).

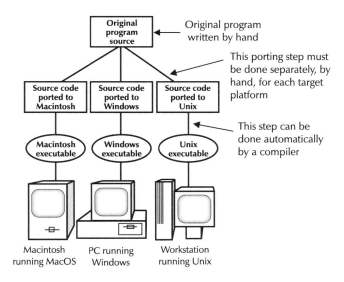

Original program written by hand

This porting step must be done separately, by hand, for each target platform

This step can be done automatically by a compiler

Figure 3.6
Multi-platform development using conventional languages

In order for traditional porting to be successful, the compilers that translate the programmer's source code into machine language for each platform must interpret the program's source code in exactly the same way. Without good source-level compatibility, the job of porting software from one platform to another is significantly more complicated. Unfortunately, the compiler marketplace is an extremely competitive one. The temptation to "extend" a language beyond ratified standards in order to give one's product an edge has proven irresistible to many compiler manufacturers.

Source-code portability is not enough—even when we can get it

A number of compiler vendors have attempted to supply versions of their compilers for multiple platforms, but these still leave the programmer with a problem: dealing with the different ways that operating systems like Windows, OS/2 Warp, the MacOS, and UNIX provide system-level services. For software to be plug-compatible the way current hardware is, we need a development system that is truly platform-independent; i.e., it must include a compiler that can target all major platforms from a single set of source code. If it can produce *executable code* that runs unchanged on all potential target platforms, so much the better: there will be no need to create multiple versions of software.

Executable code that is portable, is a better solution

Java promises this striking degree of portability across platforms by extending the concept of encapsulation to the concept of the platform. The Java system hides the computer's processor and its operating system inside a "virtual machine" (VM), which is completely abstract.

The virtual machine enables programmers to obtain system-level services like process management and graphics, yet avoid dependence on any particular operating system, by using a set of simple, generic Java class libraries designed for such tasks. It enables them to avoid dependence on a particular processor by using a form of bytecode, an intermediate language that may become a kind of computer Esperanto.

Instead of generating machine-specific instructions for an actual processor, a Java compiler produces bytecode for the virtual machine. The computers we use every day cannot execute bytecode directly. The user's machine must rely on a runtime implementation of the virtual machine, tailored to its processor type. An interpreter in the runtime system reads the Java bytecode and executes instructions native to that processor.

A Java program will run on any Java-supported system—that is, on any popular platform

Runtime interpretation of bytecode adds overhead, but, because it is similar to assembly language, performance is adequate for many applications. And, because it is not specific to any processor or operating system, bytecode is fully portable. Machines as diverse as MacOS, Windows 95, and Solaris can use exactly the same code. Java runtime systems are available for most popular processors; any Java program can run unaltered on any of them (see Figure 3.7).

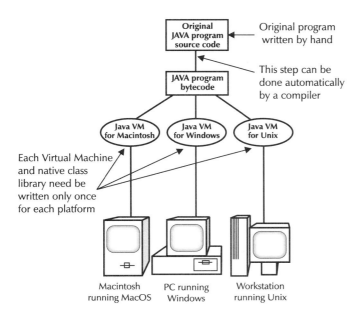

**Figure 3.7
Multi-platform
development using Java**

Original program
written by hand

This step can be
done automatically
by a compiler

Each Virtual Machine
and native class
library need be
written only once
for each platform

Macintosh
running MacOS

PC running
Windows

Workstation
running Unix

The impact of Java on platform vendors

The potential of Java's virtual machine raises troubling questions for processor manufacturers and vendors of operating systems.

Users have consistently demanded systems that let them use their old software on new platforms. Manufacturers such as Intel and Microsoft have catered to this requirement by making their newer processor and operating-system designs backward-compatible, that is, compatible with earlier products.

Backward compatibility lets users upgrade hardware, yet keep familiar software...

The IBM PC-compatible family is a perfect example of the success of backward compatibility. In terms of sheer volume, PCs based on Intel processors running Microsoft DOS, Windows, or Windows 95 represent the largest share of the desktop market. For this reason there is an abundance of applications software available for these computers—in fact, many companies buy PCs in order to run some critical application which is not available on any other platform.

Thanks to backward compatibility, a program written in 1981 for a PC with an 8088 processor and running MS-DOS can still be used unchanged on today's immensely more powerful Pentium processors running Windows 95. Users of legacy systems, older applications which are indispensable but not yet available for new computers, benefit greatly: they can purchase a computer built with any processor in the Pentium family and not worry about application compatibility.

...and hampers innovation in processors and operating systems

Benefits to vendors have not been without costs. The requirement that newer processors run the vast array of legacy software owned by most computer users has become a millstone around the necks of chip and OS manufacturers. While the Pentium Pro was designed for the new 32-bit operating systems of the 1990's, it still must support 16-bit programs from 1981. Similarly, Microsoft needed to support DOS and 16-bit Windows programs even in its latest versions of Windows NT and Windows 95.

This need for compatibility introduces complexity into design that the Java virtual machine and class libraries could eliminate. Moving compatibility questions out of the processor and into a virtual machine liberates chip and OS vendors from worries about legacy code and backward compatibility, and lets them concentrate on using available technology to extract maximum performance and functionality.

How will industry leaders be affected when hardware choice no longer dictates software choice, and vice versa?

Of course, hardware and operating system manufacturers have reason to fear Java precisely because it gives freedom to users. Instead of being locked into a single platform and being all but held captive by one or two suppliers, users will at last be free to pick and choose from a much wider range of equipment and software. Being able to choose a hardware platform without worrying about the availability of specific software packages should result in significant savings and overall performance improvements for the average computer user.

If they embrace Java, established market leaders will be opening doors to their competition. They may need to revise their strategies toward competing more aggressively on a price/performance basis, once they are no longer able to rely on their possession of de facto standards as a marketing advantage.

Communicating Tasks: Distributed Program Code

Back to the Future: HTML = Block mode '95

The rise of the Internet has made some propose the current standard for Web-page creation, Hypertext Markup Language (HTML), as a simple route to platform independence. Browsers that can interpret HTML are now available for every platform, and some Web sites implement extremely sophisticated applications using HTML forms.

The Web has resurrected an archaic communications mode

Unfortunately, while applications written in HTML present graphics and attractively formatted text, they are transmitted the same way text screens were sent to the 3270 terminals of 30 years ago. In other words, current Internet applications operate the same way that block-mode software did on the mainframe monoliths of the 60s. Web browsers like Netscape Navigator turn high-powered PCs into fancy block-mode terminals connected to larger computers through the Internet.

To illustrate the problem more concretely, imagine that a bank wants to market its mortgages by putting up a Web page that allows Internet users to work out monthly repayments associated with the different mortgage terms the bank offers. If the bank wanted to use HTML, it would implement the calculator using HTML forms, which are essentially block-mode screens, and CGI scripts, which are programs that run on the bank's Web site, not the user's computer.

The mortgage calculator might be implemented this way:

1   First the bank's computer sends a page of instructions to the browser.

2   The browser interprets these instructions and displays a screen containing a form and some instructions for the user.

3   Next, the user fills out the relevant fields on the form and clicks on a submit button, and the browser sends back the information the user entered to the bank's Web site.

4   A CGI script on the bank's computer performs the necessary calculations, then creates a new HTML page containing the results and sends it back to the user's browser for display.

So, although the user's computer may be perfectly capable of running a mortgage calculation, it does no more than display a form. While HTML allows software like the mortgage calculator to be platform-independent, it does so at a large cost to Web servers and to general Internet performance. Overloading often cripples popular sites on the Internet. When one considers that the most frequently visited sites are accessed millions of times per day, the cause of the bottlenecks becomes apparent. The dumb browser, by placing extreme pressure on processors and network bandwidth, causes the most popular segments of the Internet to become very slow—even unreachable at some times of the day.

...or the customer's? The question must be asked: Why doesn't the Web page perform the mortgage calculation on the user's own computer? It would be faster for the user, and would allow the Internet and the bank's Web site to serve many more users without needing an expensive upgrade. In fact, what is needed is a shift to the client-server model.

Client-Server and the Internet

Just as client-server technology in a single company distributes processing burdens more rationally, converting the Internet to the client-server model will allow browsers to relieve Web servers of congestion by taking on some of the necessary work. The technical problem posed by the large number of clients has so far prevented the 'net from adopting this model. Because the Internet is so vast, it is not practical for users to install a client for every program they might possibly need on their computers. We need, not only a browser that can carry some of processing load, but a browser that can adapt to changing needs by adding extra functionality.

"Dynamic browsers" can enhance themselves automatically, using a mechanism provided by the "applet" concept. An applet is a program designed specifically for loading across a network and, as such, has special attributes and restrictions applied to it. Applets are generally small programs with a single purpose. Applets can be delivered to the target machine through a direct link to a LAN or WAN, but their creators keep them small, to allow easy downloading across the potentially low-speed network connections associated with dial-up Internet access.

Dynamic browsers can enhance themselves, easily and automatically

To give a simple example: Web browsers can display images stored in Graphics Interchange Format (GIF) or Joint Photographic Experts Group format (JPEG). Suppose someone develops a new graphics format that is smaller, faster, or better in some other way than GIF or JPEG?

Users of static browsers who want to display images stored in the new format will need to hunt out an appropriate plug-in program, download it, install it, and configure their browsers appropriately. All this effort becomes unnecessary, however, if their browsers are dynamic. A display program developed in applet form can be stored with the image itself. A dynamic browser will automatically see that it needs the applet as well as the image, and download it automatically, and thereby extend its capabilities transparently (see Figure 3.8).

Platform dependence made this approach unfeasible until recently. Lacking an object-oriented, architecture-neutral language, developers wishing to make a new browser extension

Figure 3.8
A dynamic Web browser downloading a new applet automatically

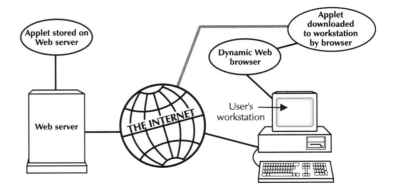

Platform independence is a sine qua non

available to the users of today's wide variety of platforms faced the daunting task of creating and supporting a large number of versions. Microsoft's ActiveX technology, for example, is designed to allow easy downloading of applications—but only by browsers running on Windows 95 and Windows NT platforms.

Java's virtual machine provides a more comprehensive, platform-independent solution to the browser-extension problem. Its widely portable applets enable dynamic browsers to enhance themselves simply and automatically on any Java-supported platform. HotJava and Netscape Navigator were only the first of many browsers that will use applets to add support for new services and features as soon as they appear on the Internet. Applets are discussed in more detail in Chapter 4.

As software comes down, system administrators' blood pressure goes up

Downloading applets from the network is a convenient way to expand functionality, but it does raise security questions. System administrators and individual users will be reluctant to install a program straight off the 'net unless its capabilities are restricted and its source can be authenticated. Giving an unknown program free access to local resources represents an unacceptable threat to the integrity and reliability of any system. Java applets differ from ActiveX applications not only in their platform independence but in the superior security support built into them. Java offers several levels of security

CHAPTER 3 • WHERE DO WE GO FROM HERE?

control for applets; selecting the maximum level affords users very high levels of protection. The details of these security methods are discussed in Chapter 8.

Java's design obviates the need for each computer to keep its own copy of every useful program. All the code needed to run an application can be downloaded as required. Just-in-time distribution has raised the question: Why not leave all the software on servers?

Several companies will soon distribute Java-based "Internet appliances," inexpensive computers that load all their application software as needed from the 'net instead of from a local hard drive. Such dynamic program distribution excites the interest of system administrators because it does away with the tedium of updating clients to new software versions. It is likely to appeal to many users, if only because it offers the prospect of renting software on a per-use basis instead of buying it outright. They may find it economical to use even the most expensive software for short periods of time, and beneficial to "test drive" programs they are considering purchasing.

"Care to take our new CAD package for a little spin around the block?"

Load Balancing: Applets and their Role in Distributed Processing

Many developers today confront the challenge of producing software systems that will distribute processing across networks composed of a wide variety of platforms. Although a number of distributed-processing environments are already on the market, they tend to narrow their focus to a single special purpose, to require all machines to be running the same platform, or both.

Take QNX as an example: this operating system makes it easy for programmers to harness the total computing power of a network in an almost transparent manner. With comparatively little effort, programmers can distribute tasks across a number of machines. One weakness is that QNX solutions

QNX demonstrates the power of conventional distributed processing— and its limitations

are limited to a single processor type. A designer cannot use QNX to create a single processing resource that comprises Apple, IBM, and Sun computers. Another limitation is that, although QNX is extremely powerful and effective when used within its intended marketplace, it is not a general-purpose operating system. It also lacks many essential personal-productivity applications, such as WYSIWYG word processing.

For distributed-processing systems to be cost-effective across a range of different computer types, they must be free of platform dependencies, and must be able to regard all the computers in a network as identical. This seemingly insurmountable hurdle may be the reason so few systems completely embrace the distributed-processing paradigm, and that designers often fall back on simpler, more rigidly defined distributions of processing tasks, such as client-server systems.

QNX demonstrates the power of conventional distributed processing— and its limitations

Dynamically distributed programs can be written in other computer languages, but Java has been designed specifically for this type of use. Its virtual-machine design inherently "regards all computers as identical." Platform independence makes it easy to develop programs that will run on every machine in a heterogenous network, and built-in network support makes it easy to distribute tasks at run time.

Java's suitability to distributed processing is only one example of its potential to bring flexibility and extensibility to computer software used across networks comprising widely different platforms. Properly exploited, Java can enable software developers to deploy the kinds of strategies hardware makers have used to cut the complexity of their systems, including "divide and conquer" and standardized interfaces. Java thus has the potential to revolutionize the way systems are designed, administered, and used.

CHAPTER 3 • WHERE DO WE GO FROM HERE?

4

Applets, A Key Component
Of The Web

 For years, denizens of the World Wide Web have used browsers like Mosaic and Netscape Navigator to explore the Internet. The sheer size and diversity of Web content has concealed a simple fact: browsers are not especially intelligent. Most do no more than present hyperlinked text and graphics, and send commands to run scripts located on the server.

Extending Browser Functionality

Recently Web browsers have expanded their functionality by incorporating new features and products. For instance, Netscape provided a plug-in mechanism to allow easy integration of small, specialized utility applications into Navigator.

Recent browser extensions have their shortcomings

This scheme does not entirely satisfy. Each different platform requires its own version of each plug-in. Furthermore, users must explicitly download and install the correct version before using it—only once, but the plethora of plug-ins inconveniences many users. And, once installed, plug-ins continue to take up space on the local disk until explicitly deleted.

Worst of all, they are woefully insecure. An off-site process can walk through the door opened by a plug-in and transmit sensitive data back to the server, destroy data and programs, or implant a virus. It can even gain surreptitious access to other systems, perhaps impersonating the unsuspecting user.

Applets offer many advantages over plug-ins

By contrast, a Java applet's operation is seamlessly integrated into the browser. A Java-powered browser automatically downloads and executes each needed applet. The user need not request these operations consciously and must look closely even to see them occur. The only obvious difference is the functionality that suddenly appears (see Figure 4.1).

Typically, the browser stores each applet in a temporary cache in the local computer's memory or disk. When its usefulness ends, the browser releases for other use the space it has occupied. Depending on local caching features and on the nature of the applet itself, space may be freed as soon as the user jumps to another Web page, or not until the browser itself terminates.

Strong security features (described in detail in Chapter 8) give applets perhaps their biggest advantage over plug-ins. They sharply reduce the risk that a non-local process can damage the user's system.

Figure 4.1
A dynamic, Java-enabled Web browser

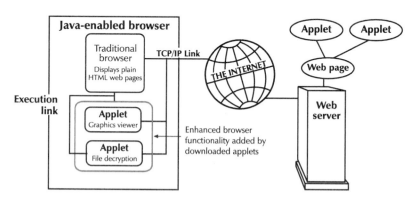

CHAPTER 4 • APPLETS, A KEY COMPONENT OF THE WEB

We know that adding programs to a browser can greatly extend its functionality. What would be the most desirable attributes of such programs? Any likely answer to that question would look like a list of the characteristics of Java applets:

Applets' features make them natural browser extenders

- ❖ Platform independence
- ❖ Small size, for quick downloading
- ❖ Multi-threading
- ❖ Strong security built in
- ❖ Inherent support for the network model

The First Applets

In Java's early days, many applets were simple implementations of the technology, intended more to demonstrate applets' capabilities than to perform any useful work. One example is the Animator, which Sun designed and included in its Java Development Kit as a demonstration.

The first applets aimed to demonstrate their potential

Arguably the most widely used applet, it is responsible for the steam rising from the coffee cup we see on Sun's own Java pages (see Figure 4.2).

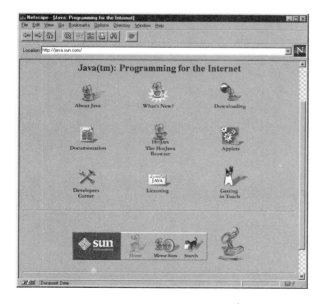

**Figure 4.2
Sun's Java home page**

Another simple animation is Duke, a tumbling cartoon character that doubles as Java's mascot (see Figure 4.3). In one demonstration, Duke cartwheels across the screen, dazzling the viewer with the energizing effect of dynamic graphics on Web pages.

Figure 4.3
Sun's Java mascot, Duke

Users can even interact with graphical images in real time

The addition of real-time user input to a graphical interface promises an exciting degree of interaction, easily seen in the X-Y vs. Time 3D Graph. This applet displays a three-dimensional plot of continually changing data, and lets the user view it from any angle by rotating it with the mouse (see Figure 4.4). The results are levels of presentation impact and interactivity impossible on static Web pages.

Figure 4.4
A three-dimensional graphing applet

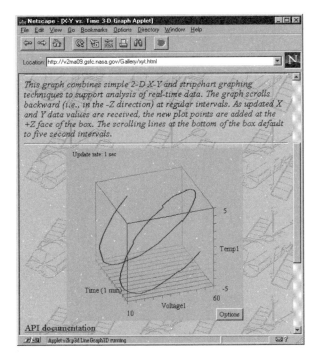

Games were also among the first applets. Many are simple, easily implemented ports of card games and classic video games. Users can play PacMan, Monopoly, Solitaire, and other games within the confines of their Web browsers. Developers have created several new games that take advantage of advanced features of the Java environment. The network-friendly nature of applets even makes it easy to create and update high-scores lists that are truly "World Wide."

Who will be the first world champion of PacMan?

The distinction between games and simulations is somewhat blurred; indeed, applets often include components of both types. Simulation applets already on the Internet demonstrate the potential to expand dramatically the Web's role as an educational medium. One grimly amusing example is a simulation of the Chernobyl nuclear reactor; players manipulate pumps, valves, and damping rods to try to prevent a nuclear meltdown (see Figure 4.5).

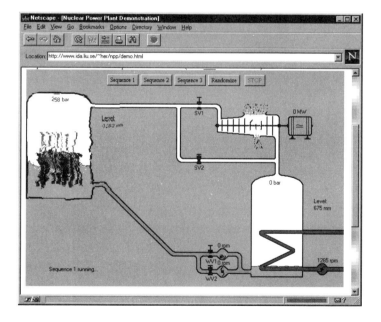

**Figure 4.5
A nuclear-reactor simulation applet**

Second-Generation Applets

More recent applets have demonstrated a capacity to do productive work

The latest applets illustrate the growing range of functionality Java programmers are discovering. As they apply advanced programming techniques and improve user interface, they also show just how practical applets can be. For example, the Wall Street Web applet keeps investors up with the market by continually updating a ticker and graphical reports on stocks they themselves select (see Figure 4.6).

Figure 4.6
A portfolio-management applet

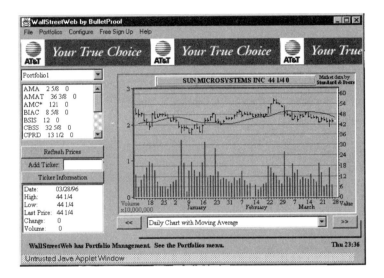

This applet provides a visual interface to a database of specific information. Its dynamic and interactive nature add a new perspective on material available through traditional online methods. The range of subjects is unlimited. For a page on human biology, an applet can provide illustrations of detailed medical data, and allow the user to rotate, zoom, and perform other operations on the image. One such applet is the Body Viewer (see Figure 4.7).

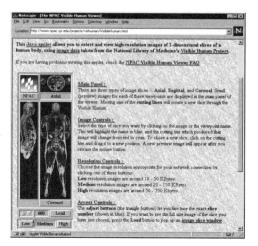

Figure 4.7
A body-viewer applet

Many second-generation applets feature multi-user interaction. Java-based chat servers allow users to share both text and graphics. For example, members of a design team separated by thousands of miles can use a "distributed whiteboard" to exchange ideas much as if they were all in a single conference room. The Multi-user White Board applet splits a window into two sections, a public drawing space and a discussion area, so participants can sketch diagrams for each other as easily as they exchange comments (see Figure 4.8).

A multi-user applet creates a virtual conference room

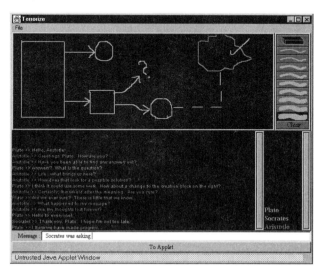

Figure 4.8
A virtual-whiteboard applet

Applets can distribute program workloads as well as user interaction

The Multi-user White Board demonstrates one exciting potential, but the possibilities do not end with distributed interaction. We can envision programs that share fundamental parts of their operation among multiple computers. A multi-player action game could demonstrate this concept: A number of separate applets, each responsible for some aspect of the game play, would run on each player's computer. These applets would handle the player input and internal computations locally, leaving to the Internet only such tasks as relaying the position and status of the individual players (see Figure 4.9).

Figure 4.9
A network-distributed multi-player game

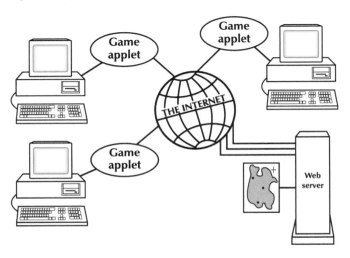

Further demonstrations of what applets can do may be found on the Web

These examples only sketch bare outlines of the capabilities inherent in Java applets now in use. The extensive list of applets and resources at Gamelan

$$\text{(http://www. gamelan.com/)}$$

paints a more complete picture. As well, the JARS site (Java Applet Rating Service, `http://www. jars.com/`) showcases many of the more impressive applets on the Web. In only the first few months development tools were available, programmers produced scores of fascinating demonstrations of Java's utility; even more exciting applets are on the horizon.

CHAPTER 4 • APPLETS, A KEY COMPONENT OF THE WEB

Applets of the Future

With thousands of programmers busy honing their Java skills in the context of an Internet that continues to grow at a meteoric rate, what new Java applets will be catching our eye?

Where will applets take us next?

General Utilities

Stronger and more functional applets will include simple, common utilities for personal use. Small word processors, graphics tools, and audiovisual utilities will enable users to manipulate text, static images, audio, and video. These applets will use data from local files and Internet documents, communicate with each other, and save new and updated files to disk just as conventional applications do. Even a small suite of such tools would be powerful enough to support Internet Appliances, a simplified, Web-based computer for the consumer market.

Smart Agents

Because Java applets integrate so neatly into a browser, we may forget that they are self-contained entities that can function independently. Because the browser can download, use, and discard them so easily and transparently, we may fail to see that applets can also remain in permanent contact with other locations on the Internet.

The Wall Street Web already demonstrates that a news service can easily display a continually updated stream of information. An even more dynamic applet would accept red-flag words and other filtering criteria, monitor a news stream, and alert the user when events of particular interest occur. For example, an investor could rely on such an applet to warn that the price of a particular stock has fallen below or risen above some preset limit. Freed of the need to "watch the ticker," the investor can concentrate on other work without losing the chance to make a timely buy or sell decision.

Read the Journal—*let an applet watch the ticker*

Another possible smart agent: an expert system in an automotive workshop could obtain and interpret information that would allow complete diagnostic analysis of a vehicle's operation. Then, before ever picking up a wrench, the mechanic could dismantle and reassemble the entire fuel-injection system on-screen, making it easy to discover the fastest way to reach the part needing repair.

Internet Commerce

Doing business over the 'net has its problems

Retail- and wholesale-level trading via the Internet may become one of the most important areas of future development—although we first must clear a number of hurdles.

Security is sure to be the most important concern. The open environment of the Internet makes it all too easy to spy on information which passes through one site on its way to another. We are likely to need a number of mechanisms to prevent mischief-makers from damaging our systems, intercepting our communications, and creating spurious or even fraudulent data in our names.

Netscape offers a "secure server" product which works with its browser to encrypt information exchanged across the Internet. (To the company's chagrin, a group of hackers quickly cracked their first implementation of this technology.) Numerous other systems have been proposed, including encryption of the TCP/IP protocol itself, but no one has yet implemented a comprehensive solution that will satisfy all parties.

Applets can help make network commerce safe

Internet vendors concerned about the integrity of security products from third parties can now use Java applets to create their own security systems—and change security methods and their implementation as required to maintain the desired level of protection. Since the applet will deliver the encryption software to the end user's machine simply in its normal course of operation, the vendor will no longer

CHAPTER 4 • APPLETS, A KEY COMPONENT OF THE WEB

need to distribute original code or updates manually. Frequent upgrades of the applet will by itself increase security of the data it transports, and vendors will retain full control over the level and methods used. Of course it is vital that the distribution method itself be secure!

At a retail level, Java applets can compose an intelligent shopping system, one that will allow users to compare prices, set maximum purchase limits, and so forth in a highly interactive manner on their own computers, rather than use the static forms and CGI-based methods now found on many Internet sites. Using simulation technology, one applet can enable prospective purchasers to examine 3D models of a product in real time, even as another determines finance charges and monthly payments for credit purchases.

Soon, no doubt, an insurance company will use expert-systems applets to help prospects select the policies most suitable to their specific needs, transmit transaction details and credit information to the company, and produce personalized policy forms on their own printers.

But can an applet put its foot in the doorway?

Some of these advanced applets will rely on future versions of client software and development tools. Netscape and Microsoft have promised to enhance their browsers in many ways to improve the security, performance, and functionality of applets. Sun has also committed to several new additions to the Java environment that will make it more useful for practical applications. The combined efforts of these companies and Java programmers themselves suggest a bright outlook for applet development.

FaxMail, a Case Study

We can get a deeper understanding of applets' capabilities by examining in detail a Java project undertaken by FaxMail Technologies. Their fax-to-electronic-mail service uses applets to support a nonstandard graphic file format in a portable way.

FaxMail addresses a problem: how to make a nonstandard data format portable

The fax-to-email service receives faxes on a computer, then converts them into highly compressed image files. It then forwards each file to the recipient as an attachment to an email message, or holds it at FaxMail's Web site until, using a browser, the recipient connects to the site and enters a unique identification and password (see Figure 4.10).

Figure 4.10
The FaxMail applet, for viewing faxes transmitted in a proprietary format

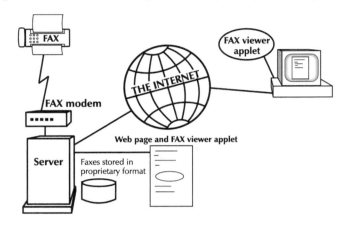

The company solved a size problem...

FaxMail realized early that fax images place huge demands on storage. Uncompressed, a typical page may use up 500 kilobytes. Existing image-compression standards such as GIF and JPEG allow reduction to a range between 60 and 120 KB, but developers considered even these sizes unacceptable. Demands on server storage would be much too large, and bandwidth limitations would slow transmission to a crawl.

To address these problems, FaxMail programmers developed new compression algorithms and a storage format especially optimized for handling fax images. The result was a system that stores a full page of faxed text in just 12 to 15 KB, a saving of 80 per cent or more.

...and created a portability problem

Of course, even the best solutions create new problems: If its users were to display images in the new, nonstandard format, FaxMail needed to distribute a specialized decompression program. To reach the widest possible mar-

CHAPTER 4 • APPLETS, A KEY COMPONENT OF THE WEB

ket they would need to create a different version of the program for every popular user platform. The company could reduce distribution costs and effort by distributing the program electronically, but users would need to devote time and attention to downloading the program at least once and to running it each time they wanted to view their faxes. The process still appeared unappealingly complicated.

To get around these problems, FaxMail developed a Java applet that does all the work of decompressing and displaying images in the new format, and simply added it to the relevant Web page. Any subscriber with a Java-capable Web browser can view faxes on-screen more quickly and economically than traditional static-browser systems would allow.

An applet provided portability—and other benefits

Development costs were minimal because Java is platform-independent: a single version of the software runs on any platform with a Java interpreter. Moreover, distribution is fully automatic; the entire loading and activation of the applet is virtually transparent to the user.

To save fax images to disk and convert them to other graphical formats, or to view faxes delivered as email attachments, users will need to run FaxMail's stand-alone Java application (still under development at this writing). Adding these or other complex functions to the applet would expand it to a size that would render it unusable by those with simple dial-up connections.

Nevertheless, a single Java applet has enabled FaxMail to develop and use a totally new format for data, and yet come to market quickly, avoiding the significant costs and delays that are inevitable if one must develop a half dozen versions of the same product just to be competitive.

FaxMail's applet got to market quickly—and created an easy upgrade path

What is most striking is that FaxMail remains free to enhance its software—even to modify or replace the fax-compression format itself— without worrying about effects on older versions of their own product. The latest version of the applet downloads each time a user connects to FaxMail's Web site, ensuring that data and code are synchronized.

Automatic downloading benefits users in other ways as well: They always work with the most current release of the program but avoid the tedium of successive installation efforts. And switching platforms either temporarily or permanently is all but painless—no need to obtain a different version of the product, no need to endure minor but annoying variations among versions.

The bottom line: Java saved 30 per cent

FaxMail's switch from C++ entailed significant retooling and reskilling costs. Even after these are accounted for, however, the company estimates that using Java saved it around 30 percent of the costs of other options.

This case study is just one real-world example of how Java applets can dramatically enhance the Internet's power and ease of use.

5

Beyond Applets

 By now, Java's suitability for the creation of applets should be obvious. The benefits it offers in a networked or distributed environment more than justify the costs of upgrading skills and retooling. It would be easy to argue that its unique combination of features make Java the only practical choice for applet implementation. But is that Java's only niche? Or do those same features make it useful for the development of full-scale applications as well?

Is Java suitable for full-scale applications as well as applets?

The answer to this interesting question is critical to the long-term future of Java. We have already discussed Java's capabilities as a clean, architecture-neutral, object-oriented language. Ultimately it will be the developers that decide whether these characteristics will find Java a permanent home in the world of large-scale software development. They are the ones most likely to gain from a move to Java, at least initially.

Consumers, by contrast, are interested only in receiving a cost-effective solution to their computing requirements. At this stage, they are unconcerned with the underlying technical merits or long-term benefits of a technology such as Java. They have different priorities: a new system must perform the required tasks efficiently and effectively, work well with other systems they use, and come in at reasonable cost. A

Users will not lead the march toward Java

product's implementation language is not their choice; it is transparent to them and, superficially at least, of no consequence. Given this situation, the consumer market will become aware of Java and demand its use only if developers are able to translate its powerful features into some tangible benefit consumers can see and appreciate.

Even software developers will need some convincing

Software developers themselves derive benefits more directly than consumers or users, but still need to satisfy themselves that these will be substantial enough to justify the costs and effort of adopting the new technology. Ideally, they will perform a formal cost-benefit analysis, perhaps taking on a small pilot project to generate the necessary data. Even a pilot project entails significant expense, however. Managers need some confidence beforehand that the new technology will solve more problems than it creates.

This chapter reviews managers' key concerns and describes how Java addresses them, beginning with a feature-by-feature comparison of Java with other technologies.

The Java Face-Off

In Table 5.1, we compare Java with three of the most commonly used programming languages, C, C++, and Visual Basic, rating them on criteria of the highest interest to software development managers.

TABLE 5.1				
ATTRIBUTE	**JAVA**	**C++**	**C**	**VISUAL BASIC**
Architecture-neutrality	Yes	No	No	No
Security	Excellent	None	None	None
Built-in network support	Very good	None	None	None
OOPS support	Excellent	Very good	Poor	Poor
Language safety	Excellent	Moderate	Poor	Good
Runtime performance	Moderate/excellent[1]	Very good	Excellent	Moderate
Compile times	Very good	Poor	Moderate	Very good
Learning curve	Moderate	Hard	Moderate	Easy
Syntactical simplicity	Very good	Very poor	Good	Very good
Source portability	Excellent[2]	Moderate	Good	None
Industry acceptance	Very good	Excellent	Excellent	Very good[3]
Large-project suitability	Good	Good	Poor	Poor
Open standard	No[4]	No[5]	Yes	No
Base toolset costs	Free/low	Low	Low	Low
Base toolset functionality	Very good	Poor	Poor	Good
Third-party libraries	Moderate[6]	Excellent	Excellent	Excellent

[1]*Java performs moderately fast when interpreted, but compares well with C when fully compiled*

[2]*Portability is built into the Java language and is automatically applicable to source code unless native methods are used*

[3]*Visual Basic is available on Windows platforms only*

[4]*Java standardization efforts are planned*

[5]*C++ is in the process of becoming an open standard*

[6]*The Java community is rapidly providing equivalents to the mature libraries of other languages*

From this comparison, only a fool would conclude that, overnight, Java will entirely displace other languages, as each has its own strengths as well as weaknesses.

Older languages will continue to dominate some niches...

C will continue to dominate the development of smaller applications that require excellent runtime efficiencies, or which incorporate a body of legacy code.

C++ will continue to be a force in very large systems with complex object relationships. There, programmers can take better advantage of complex OOPS mechanisms such as multiple inheritance that Java has chosen to forsake in favor of elegance and simplicity. Many who have managed to grasp its sometimes awkward syntax and inconsistencies will continue to choose C++, at least when architecture-neutrality is not an essential issue.

For some time, Visual Basic will continue its role as the leading prototyping and development tool for small-scale, vertical-market software for the Microsoft Windows environment.

...but Java will find its own niches, and compete strongly for others

In each case, however, the language dominates only a particular niche in the market. Outside its niche, each is vulnerable to competition from the others, and from new entrants like Java.

From our comparison we can predict continued success for all three—and almost as safely predict that in the near future Java will become a mainstream programming language. It is already carving itself a unique niche, and that niche is in the most explosive area of the software market—indeed the one most likely to reshape the market itself. As Java matures and developers gain experience, its extraordinary combination of features, its ease of use, and its wide applicability will make it an increasingly strong competitor.

Developer Support

To succeed, Java needs strong support from third parties—developers of object libraries and development tools. That support began to appear astonishingly early. Major players like IBM, Borland, and Symantec started investing heavily in Java tools and development systems in 1995. Soon, smaller companies and even individuals followed suit.

Java development requires good support, and is getting it

Availability of high-quality, professional development tools was the first step in creating a developer community committed to using Java.

Sun got the game off to a fast start by offering its Java Developer's Kit (JDK) free through the Internet, thereby side-stepping a Catch-22 that commonly besets new languages: compiler vendors waiting for demand before producing tools, users waiting for tools before committing to the new language. Well before its 1.0 version was released, developers all over the world plunged into alpha and beta versions of the JDK in a rush to get to know the language.

Early tools reached programmers' hands quickly

Buoyed by the broad groundswell of interest among developers, compiler vendors have since been rushing to produce their own implementations. A few soon offered complete integrated development environments (IDEs) that included faster compilers, debuggers, and other tools.

Like Sun, they fed Java's burgeoning popularity by making early versions of "soon-to-be-commercial" products freely available: Borland offered a beta version of its Java debugger while it prepared more extensive development tools. Symantec made an early extension of its C/C++ IDE available for downloading through the Internet, and released a complete IDE for Java development soon after.

The Internet was vital to the rapid rise of Java's star. Broad dissemination of information and early implementations led quickly to widespread awareness and intense curiosity among programmers around the globe. If Java does fulfill its promise of becoming a mainstream language, laurels can be laid at the feet of its creators, who recognized the Internet's potential to reach a huge percentage of the developer community.

Is Anyone Actually Using Java?

The industry held back at first

In the first year after its release, how many organizations used Java to develop full-sized applications? Not many. Even though the computer industry is not renowned for its conservatism, most players adopted a "wait and see" attitude. Given the costs of retooling and retraining programmers and the immaturity of the technology, such restraint was prudent.

Early on, the lack of fully implemented compilers and the low speed of Java executables—adequate for applets but not for major programs—made it only sensible to heed one of the industry's rules of thumb: "Never trust a release zero product." Sun itself openly predicted that Java would not be ready for industrial-strength development much before the end of 1996.

A few companies tested the waters; many recalled past disappointments

For some time, most software houses and information technology departments were reluctant to spend more than modest amounts of time and money evaluating Java. A few went so far as to conduct small in-house projects as learning tools for developers and evaluation tools for management. Many others held off entirely, watching the media make all too much mileage out of any mention of the new "wonder language," which all too often prompted an "it's too good to be true" attitude among IT managers. They had seen it before—hot new products that were set to change the face of the industry but eventually faded into obscurity.

Without hard knowledge of its capabilities, it is easy to see why skeptics saw Java as the latest in a series of such nine-day wonders.

Enthusiasts pointed out that Java promises the productivity boom of object-oriented programming, but unlike C++, prevents storage leaks by managing dynamic memory automatically, replaces bug-prone pointers with simple direct references, checks for out-of-range array subscripts, uses dynamic linking to eliminate long rebuilding cycles—all of which can reduce the time programmers spend writing, testing, and fixing code—and the skeptics turned the page.

The gulf between the past promise of OOPS and the present reality still yawned in their minds. Pundits had promoted OOPS as the answer to all of the problems which plague software developers, yet too few OOPS implementations had come close to matching the claims of order-of-magnitude productivity gains. In view of the Java media circus, cynicism was understandable.

That the IT industry consists of individuals and small firms as well as giant companies can actually reduce the cost of experimenting with Java. A growing number of consultants and contract programmers are investing in their own careers by learning Java (each of the present authors knows at least four such), and companies can hire in these skills for modest explorations of Java's potential. Managers need not retrain full-time staff until their confidence in Java is higher—at which time those same third parties may serve as mentors.

Companies can benefit from the self-training of freelancers

After assessing the costs and risks, a few companies have embraced Java as the language of tomorrow. Indeed, some are developing almost exclusively in or for the Java environment. Dimension X has released a series of tools designed to blend Java with Virtual Reality Modeling Language (VRML) technology to provide dynamic and interactive virtual environments. EarthWeb, another strong Java development firm, has teamed with ACTV Inc. to deliver direct, television-synchronized video broadcasts on the Web through the HyperTV service.

These companies have jumped out to the head of what they believe will be a large and successful parade of Java development. Their vision can become a reality if, unlike the panaceas of the past, Java can actually keep the promises it has made.

What Types of Applications are Suited to Java?

Java is best suited to applications that need its strongest features

The most suitable applications for the Java environment at this writing are those that rely least on runtime performance, and that benefit most from platform independence. Examples include accounting tools, database front-ends in client-server environments, workgroup products, and PIMs/schedulers.

Networking applications, which can take advantage of Java's security features and underlying network support, are also fitting candidates. Sun has led the move toward such applications by developing the HotJava browser and the Java Workshop IDE entirely in the Java language.

Other vendors have bolstered their line-up of development products with authoring and debugging tools for Java programs.

We cannot expect to see computation-intensive applications written in Java, however, until native-code, just-in-time (JIT) compilers (Discussed in Chapter 6.) appear on all Java-supported platforms. Even then, developers will continue to code much of that software in FORTRAN, C, or C++. Likewise, certain design aspects of Java restrict its use on some legacy platforms, such as MS-DOS. As long as developers view these platforms as viable markets, they may choose to continue to program in older languages.

Improved implementations will drive an expanding range of Java-driven products

As Java moves out of its infancy, we can expect to see faster, more efficient implementations of the Java Virtual Machine (VM) for a growing number of platforms, and a proliferation of class libraries offering a dazzling range of modular functionality that moves us another step closer to the ultimate OOPS ideal. Many of these new products will be from inno-

CHAPTER 5 • BEYOND APPLETS

vative third parties, seeking to make profits and gain a foothold in the emerging software-component marketplace.

Enterprise Network Connectivity

Java should play a unique role in the development of structures and tools that support intranets: corporate networks designed around Internet technology. Java's blithe unconcern about platform dependencies makes it a natural for cross-platform support of in-house projects. A single set of executables would run on every major platform in a network, drastically reducing the time spent porting applications.

Java will find its warmest welcome on networks

Class libraries and standards are appearing that will handle the databases and legacy systems so common to enterprise networks. Sun's JDBC database-access application programming interface (API), slated for full release in the second half of 1996, features a set of Java classes. These are designed to provide a consistent mechanism for accessing existing databases, using open standards like SQL or proprietary methods like Microsoft's ODBC. This API will help companies incorporate Java into the existing framework of their intranets, and the scope and utility of Java applications themselves will expand as more such products become available.

We can expect to see new tools for interconnectivity on enterprise networks from Sun and other sources. Many will adhere to the CORBA (Common Object Request Broker Architecture) standard, developed by the Object Management Group consortium to support distribution of objects over networks. CORBA-compliant objects make requests and receive responses from an Object Request Broker (ORB); details about the server that does the actual work are transparent, hence unimportant. Theoretically, such an object can obtain services from any other complying object in any application, under any operating system, on any computer, anywhere. With Java implementing the interaction between

Java is a natural choice for the Object Request Broker movement

the applications, client-server interoperation becomes easier and more effective.

One core component of CORBA is the Interface Definition Language (IDL) standard, which defines remote interfaces. Sun has developed a Java mapping to the IDL, so applets and applications can communicate with each other and with non-Java objects by way of an ORB. A complementary tool, the Java Remote Method Invocation (RMI) system, supports definition of remote interfaces and invocation of remote methods. With these technologies, Java offers greater networking functionality on systems where interoperability is often critical to business success. It stands poised to take a strong position within the future of enterprise networks.

Applying Multiple Features

Java's success depends not on any one feature, but the combination of them

If Java makes it to the limelight on the stage of general applications development, it will not do so by relying on platform independence alone. It will be the confluence of many features that enables Java to become the language of choice.

Platform independence provides enormous flexibility, but by itself has not proved to be sufficient in the past. Several implementations of COBOL, UCSD Pascal, and others have all relied on a virtual machine (VM) approach like Java's to reduce or eliminate the need for platform-dependent code or compilation, with limited effect.

Source for other languages could end up as Java bytecode

It is possible that compilers for some popular languages could produce bytecode the Java VM can read. Naturally, languages similar to Java—ones that are modular, strongly typed, and object-oriented—are the likeliest candidates. Ada-to-Java compilation in particular has excited some interest and effort, and Visual Basic is another possibility. If this process becomes common, it should be relatively easy to port large bases of existing software to the Java environment. It may also save companies the cost of retraining programmers already skilled in other languages.

One thorny problem may arise: the design of Java bytecode has been optimized to facilitate implementation of constructs created by Java programs, and to support Java's all-important security features. In some cases runtime performance may degrade to unacceptable levels.

The elegant simplicity of the Java language is in itself very attractive. C and C++ programmers often must struggle with subtle side effects and elusive bugs. A language that is easy to learn and that eliminates whole categories of errors—some of them the most frustrating to trace—is very alluring indeed.

Friends and Foes

Some hardware vendors will be very keen to see Java succeed as a tool for general applications development because it will increase the range of software available for their own systems. By the same token, some industry giants may well see Java as a significant threat to their current dominance. Perhaps Microsoft will work hard to reposition Visual Basic as a platform-independent competitor to Java, or produce some other offering in an attempt to hold its high ground. Either way, the marketing muscle of present industry leaders could have enormous impact on Java's success or failure as a mainstream programming language.

Some will see Java as a promise, others as a threat

It is fair to say that neither platform independence, nor built-in security, nor multi-threading support, nor object orientation, nor any of Java's other features alone would be enough to justify a move away from existing languages. Putting all of them into one package, however, provides a powerful reason to choose Java as a mainstream applications development tool.

A closer look behind the glowing pictures painted by the first explorers of this new programming territory reveals the abundance of potential that Java offers to developers and consumers. This chapter has provided glimpses of the pioneers who have already begun realizing that potential, and have made it easier for the settlers who will follow. With so much early success in its favor, it is very hard to imagine how Java could fail.

6

Performance

Even ardent boosters of a language must be willing to confront its limitations. Perhaps the most common criticism of Sun's earliest Java implementations was that the executables they produced were not very fast. This lackluster performance had two causes—the overhead required to implement some of Java's features and, more fundamentally, Java's use of virtual-machine technology.

The Virtual Machine

Most modern programming languages are "fully compiled;" for example, a C++ compiler translates the instructions the programmer writes (the "source code") directly into instructions specific to a particular processor (its "native code"). The processor can execute these instructions very rapidly because it is "reading in its own language;" after compilation, no further translation is necessary. The downside of this strategy is that the executable form of the program can run only on that one kind of machine, and developers must use a different compiler to produce a different executable for every kind of target machine. Source code may be portable, but executable code is not.

The tradeoff: fully compiled code is faster, but not portable

By contrast, every Java executable *is* portable. A Java compiler remains blissfully ignorant of the architecture of any given processor; its target is not a real computer, but rather a virtual machine (VM). It produces, not machine instructions specific to a particular processor, but compact bytecode instructions. Each time the program is run, a Java interpreter reads the Java bytecode and executes instructions native to that processor.

The tradeoff: bytecode is portable, but continual interpretation slows processing

The interpreter cannot be architecture-neutral, of course—but, for any given processor, creating a single VM implementation that will run any Java program is much simpler than reimplementing every application. This flexibility makes cross-platform development much easier, but at a cost: interpretation causes Java programs to run slower than fully compiled programs.

This chapter assesses the magnitude of this cost, estimates the level of concern it should properly raise, describes ways it may be ameliorated, and discusses its impact on Java's suitability to particular projects.

Background

A tongue-in-cheek dictum of the computer business states that the "Big Four" uses of computers are word processing, databases, spreadsheets, and word processing.

Faster computers have led to more functional programs, written in high-level languages

Just a decade ago, when the average desktop computer had a fiftieth of the power we find in today's mid-range PCs, software performance was crucial. The Big Four applications all ran in character mode and had small, simple feature sets, yet pushed the machines to the limit. Early versions of WordPerfect were written entirely in assembly language because that was their only way to get decent performance out of the machines of the time. The first "advanced" graphical versions of venerable favorites sacrificed desirable functionality to achieve speed that was barely acceptable. Even so, many customers shunned them because the only machines that could run them at all were priced out of reach.

Today, however, computers have power to burn for doing traditional Big Four tasks. While users type into a word-processing document or enter data into a spreadsheet, their machines actually have little to do. Only a few programs tax the power of the average desktop computer to its limits. With capacity to spare, developers are free to enrich the feature sets of their products, and to use high-level languages to increase their own productivity.

The UCSD-P system offered in the early 1980s the platform independence Java offers today. It, too, produced an intermediate representation to be interpreted by a virtual machine (VM)—but by the middle of the decade it had all but disappeared. Why did it fail? One reason was that computers of the day simply could not cope with the performance penalties a VM interpreter imposed on them, and the benefits gained were an inadequate tradeoff.

Java enthusiasts should keep the history of P-code in mind

Some naysayers believe the Java VM is doomed to the same fate, but Java has two advantages its predecessor did not: it came along at a time when available power is generous enough to be forgiving; and its unique combination of features offers far more benefits than simple platform independence.

Relative Performance

In this section, we compare Java's performance to that of other mainstream languages, and investigate the differences we discover.

The following graph (Figure 6.1) summarizes results of benchmark tests of execution speed for Java and other popular programming languages.

Figure 6.1
Comparing performance: raw computation

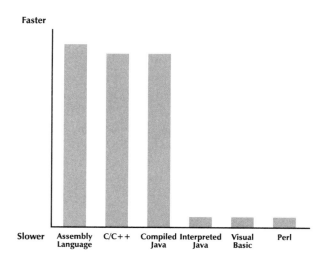

"Lies, damnable lies, and statistics"—Mark Twain

Any language's strengths and weaknesses suit it better to some applications than others, of course, but on average we can expect that a computation-intensive Java application will run a twentieth as fast the same program written in C or C++. Knee-jerk reactions to numbers like this one are common among people who forget that benchmarks are just statistics, and that 84.7 per cent of all statistics are made up. It is all too easy to focus on only a small part of the overall picture. Comparing modern GUI versions of Big Four applications may give us a more accurate view (see Figure 6.2).

Figure 6.2
Comparing performance: GUI application

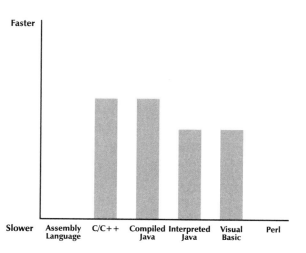

CHAPTER 6 • PERFORMANCE

The speed differences drop sharply. Why?

The answer lies in the interactive nature of most desktop applications. Much of the time they do nothing but wait for a keystroke or a mouse click. Because they are not executing instructions, efficient use of the processor is irrelevant. A program not executing native code has no performance advantage over a program not executing bytecode!

Computers are fast; people are slow

If we think about the applications we use every day—word processor, spreadsheet, database, appointment scheduler—honesty obliges us to admit that the biggest constraint on their performance is our own typing speed. Raw speed is unimportant until we run a program that does statistical analysis, 3D rendering, or some other computationally bound task, and the performance advantage of a fully compiled program makes less difference to us.

Another factor that affects a program's actual performance is the proportion of its work it can delegate to lower-level systems.

Low-level libraries ease the performance burden

Modern operating systems, sophisticated file systems, and graphical user interfaces feature rich libraries of routines that do much of the detail work once left to applications. These routines are usually heavily optimized, and in any case run at a speed that does not depend on the nature of the application that invokes them. The time spent executing them is often a sizable fraction of a program's total load on the processor. The higher this percentage, the less important the speed of the application's own code becomes.

Java programs are not the only ones that rely on partial interpretation. Significant portions of Microsoft applications like Word and Excel use their own form of bytecode in an internal VM system, yet perform satisfactorily. (The company's objective was not portability, but reduced code size: bytecode can be designed to make far more efficient use of available storage than native code does.)

Interpreted languages are more common than we may believe

Visual Basic (VB), perhaps the most popular development system for Microsoft Windows-based applications, also relies on a semi-interpreted design. Despite this apparent handicap, VB developers produce a wide range of commercial-grade software. Because most Windows applications are highly interactive, the performance issue seldom arises.

Garbage Collection

Like its reliance on a virtual machine, Java's automated garbage collection contributes to the perception that Java is "performance-challenged."

Even good programs generate garbage—bits of memory that must be recycled

The adage "garbage in, garbage out" reminds us that even the best programs produce results only as good as the input given to them. It may surprise some that even those "best programs" can generate their own kind of garbage. At run time, a program uses a fragment of the computer's memory to hold each datum. When the datum is of no further use, the space it occupies is useless waste. This "garbage" can be recycled for future use. The question is: Who should collect it?

Many languages, including Pascal, C, and C++, take no responsibility for tidying up the mess obsolete data leave behind. They rely on programmers to collect garbage manually. For each source line that allocates memory, there should be another that explicitly releases it for other use. This arrangement has one big advantage: it spares processor cycles the computer would use to discover whether any wasted memory could be reclaimed.

Manual garbage collection is tedious and error-prone—and hurts performance

The downside is that programmers aren't perfect; like teenagers, they often forget to tidy up properly. Such omissions can cause a huge variety of bugs, subtle and not so subtle, that often do not appear until after the product is shipped. Manual garbage collection often increases an application's complexity, which in turn increases development costs. It also reduces execution speed, the principal benefit manual garbage collection should achieve.

Java's designers took the other road, deciding that automatic garbage collection would provide programming simplicity and reliability that justified the reduced performance that could result. The language definition specifically requires implementations of the virtual machine to collect garbage automatically.

In its early releases, Sun's garbage collection was rather slow, probably because the mechanisms chosen were relatively simple to put in place. As Java enters the mainstream, however, application developers will demand strong real-time performance, and toolmakers must choose more sophisticated algorithms from the wide selection of garbage-collection technology available.

Automatic garbage collection can be fast

Multiple Threads of Control

The users' perception of a program's speed is more important than numbers in a table or a bar on a graph. If developers can make the program respond in timely fashion, it will satisfy users even if the methods chosen actually increase total processing time.

Threads increase perceived performance

An increasingly common way to improve perceived performance is multi-threading—having a program perform two or more tasks simultaneously, much as a modern operating system enables multiple programs to run concurrently. A database program can illustrate this concept: A single-threaded version of it will prevent the user from entering new data while a report is printing, or bar printing while it updates the database. A multi-threaded version of the same program will allow the user to enter new information while earlier entries are written out to disk, and to do both while a report is printing. Even if it uses extra processor time to provide concurrency, users will perceive it to be a fast program because it never makes them wait.

Java supports multi-threading, and does so with methods superior to those of other languages. Some C and C++

compilers provide means for the programmer to create and control multiple threads manually. These often rely on system-level libraries, however, and the result is platform-specific code. Java's support for multi-threading is built into the language, so it is fully portable and much easier for programmers to use.

Getting the best performance out of Java programs obliges the programmer to understand the capabilities and limitations of the language, and to design accordingly. Intelligent use of multi-threading and other Java features can reduce substantially the perceived performance difference between Java and its fully compiled peers.

Can we go further? Are there ways to improve not only perceived performance but raw performance as well, and make Java's execution speed fully comparable to that of other languages?

Performance Options

As developers of Java tools improve their ability to optimize Java applications and applets, raw performance of these programs will continue to improve. This trend was evident soon after the first implementations of Java became available. For example, Symantec's first implementation of the Java virtual machine performed about twice as well as Sun's earliest offerings.

Compiling "Just In Time"

We can never completely close the speed gap, however, as long as an interpreter performs runtime translation. It is possible to build Java compilers that produce platform-specific code, as C/C++ compilers do. Java programs would then execute as fast as, if not faster than, C/C++ programs. But is there a way to get this kind of speed without sacrificing one of Java's main benefits, architecture neutrality?

Just-in-time (JIT) compilers can take us off the horns of this dilemma. We can replace the Java interpreter with a second compiler, one that resides on the user's machine. Developers continue to distribute Java programs in the same fully portable bytecode form. Like the interpreter, the extra compiler translates the bytecodes into machine-specific instructions, but before execution rather than throughout run time. The second compilation causes a delay, but only a short one, because the first compiler has already handled the time-consuming parsing tasks. Now, fully compiled, the program runs as fast as a C or C++ program.

Just-in-time compilation combines the flexibility of an interpreter with the speed of a compiler

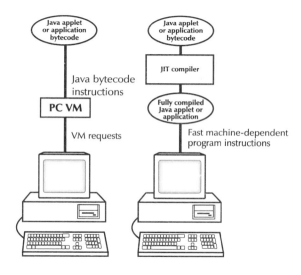

Figure 6.3
Interpretation vs. just-in-time compilation

The beauty of it is this: the just-in-time compiler is part of the Java runtime system rather than the development system, so we retain platform independence; yet, the running program is in native code, so we achieve the execution speed we feared we had lost forever.

Recent implementations of the Java virtual machine show notable performance increases, but the future may belong to (JIT) compilers. All of the major commercial Java development tool vendors are producing them, and benchmark tests reveal execution speeds for JIT-compiled Java programs indistinguishable from those of C and C++ programs.

The Java Chip

Java on a chip?

If the goal is sheer, blinding speed, why stop at a compiler? Why not build a Java-specific processor, one in which the bytecode *is* the machine code? A processor that executes Java bytecodes directly eliminates the overhead of the second translation step entirely. A "Java chip" dispenses with both the virtual machine and the JIT compiler, and could conceivably increase execution speeds by an order of magnitude.

Limitations inherent in current processor technology should restrain overconfidence about speed gains we can realistically expect from a Java chip. A full-blown JIT compiler running on a general-purpose processor can perform extensive and comprehensive optimizations. By contrast, a Java chip will have only enough capacity to optimize small, highly localized chunks of code as they stream through the processor, unless the processor itself has unusually large amounts of on-chip memory.

Small-scale optimization is relatively straightforward, yet can improve speeds by a factor of 10 or more in chips no more sophisticated than the ones available today—whether we choose the chip or the JIT compiler. To achieve significantly greater gains, a Java chip will need to "push out the edge of the envelope" of processor technology, and will thus be difficult and expensive to develop. JIT compilers that perform large-scale optimizations, on the other hand, could conceivably speed execution by a factor near thirty, without straining at the boundaries of current art.

Should we conclude that Java chips are a dead end? Not at all.

Java's original mission was to power consumer-electronics devices. Many of its features made it attractive for embedded systems, but one problem seemed insurmountable: it would be hard to make either an interpreter or a JIT compiler small enough to fit within embedded systems' severe memory constraints. Moving Java's runtime functionality to a separate chip could remove this barrier. Since embedded devices typically perform highly specialized tasks, the lack of memory a general-purpose processor requires is less of a concern.

Java chips can bring OO technology to consumer electronic devices

There is another reason why we are more likely to see Java chips in embedded devices than in larger systems.

Customers demand more and more functionality from every kind of product, but they are not disappointed if an embedded device limits enhancements largely to its own area of specialty. Users expect desktop machines to be completely open-ended, however; they want to be free to run the latest software of every kind from the broadest possible range of vendors. They may be satisfied if their new screenphone plays a cheerful little tune while it transfers money from one bank account to another—but they will expect their new PC to *compose* tunes while it performs what-if analysis on next year's budget.

Users find that kind of flexibility in today's systems, because their general-purpose processors run software written in almost every popular language. By its very definition, however, a Java chip will run only Java bytecode, limiting the user's choices to programs written in Java.

Users' insistence on software choice may limit the appeal of large systems driven by Java chips

Two sad examples from the past ought to temper optimism that there will be a big market for Java-specific processors driving large, general-purpose systems: In the early 1980s, a processor was developed to execute the UCSD-P code popular at the time; despite glowing predictions of success, that chip and the UCSD-P system itself faded into obscurity. Lisp machines met a similar fate. Both placed demands on hardware that the machines of the day simply could not handle, and neither attracted enough developers of mainstream applications to satisfy a broad market. These cautionary tales do not predict failure for the Java chip, but they do imply limits on its range of suitability.

They also constitute a useful reality check amid the wild claims that always seem to herald any exciting new technology. Java-chip technology has the potential to improve execution speeds many times over, but only time will tell where and how it will be profitably applied.

The Right Tool for the Job

Just how much performance is enough? This question is crucial when considering any language's suitability to a particular project. As is ever the case, the answer depends on the nature of the application and the constraints within which it must operate, and developers must weigh the language's strengths and weaknesses against these concerns honestly.

"There ain't no such thing as a free lunch"

Voluminous hyperbole to the contrary, Java is no silver bullet: it is not the best choice for every kind of application. We must acknowledge that interpreted Java is fully an order of magnitude slower than compiled code. On the other hand, we have seen that rapid execution isn't always necessary; that designing the system to capitalize on strengths like built-in multi-threading can reduce its reliance on simple execution speed; and that—with the arrival of better interpreters, (JIT) compilers, and Java chips—Java's performance can only improve.

7

Productivity

In any development team, every member—coder, analyst, manager, executive, or shareholder—knows that everyone's future depends on productivity, and considers it a crucial factor when considering adoption of new technology. This chapter assesses the impact various aspects of Java can have on productivity.

Measuring Productivity

How do we measure productivity in a development environment? What is it that we consider to be the end result of the programming process? These questions and many more that follow from them have created an entire field of study in computer science.

Productivity measurement is a complex, contentious field of study in computer science

Traditionally, productivity has been measured by counting the lines of finished source code programmers produced in a day. Research has discredited this approach as too susceptible to variations in language and individual programmer style. If a morning's revision shortens a 50-line routine to 30 and improves its efficiency, has the programmer been negatively productive?

More recent approaches have resulted in elaborate families of techniques with their own vocabulary, featuring such arcane terms as "cyclomatic complexity" and "function points." Use of these techniques across the industry as a whole has been sketchy.

In a larger view, the real measure of productivity is the product

Ultimately, though, productivity must be measured by the total cost required to produce a well-designed, intelligently coded, fully tested, thoroughly debugged, and carefully documented product, ready to ship on time. Our discussion will not focus narrowly on the minute-by-minute work of coders, but rather on the larger scope of impact Java can have on nearly every part of the software development process.

Java Productivity Features

Gains from Object Orientation

Java is a strongly typed, dynamically bound, object-oriented language. Many of its mechanisms for implementing the OO paradigm were designed with developer productivity in mind.

Java supports all of the productivity-enhancing features of OO

It generates all of the benefits commonly claimed for OOPS, and in a tighter, cleaner, and simpler manner than others. Encapsulation reduces complexity; inheritance, polymorphism, and delegation increase code reuse. Together they reduce dramatically the effort that must be expended throughout the analysis, design, implementation, testing, and maintenance phases of the software development life cycle.

But why have so few OO development projects attained these often-promised benefits? They have failed because these benefits depend to a great extent on the presence of a well-designed, robust, feature-laden, thoroughly tested class library that is too often absent, particularly in companies that have only recently begun using C++. Youthful as it is, Java offers a richer library of off-the-shelf classes, although it cannot yet compare with a mature OO system like SmallTalk.

Developing a class library, or enriching one, is a good way to develop Java skills, but it is important not to waste time reinventing the wheel. Creating collection classes is a good exercise, but ultimately not very productive: these classes are already widely available. New Java programmers can achieve much the same educational benefit, and much greater economic leverage, by constructing classes specific to their own business area, classes they can later use again and again when developing actual products. It will be this ability to reuse classes that will produce the return on investment promised by OO pundits.

We cannot reuse code we never write in the first place

Gains From Platform Independence

Among popular object-oriented languages, only Java can add the tremendous productivity gains to be had from architecture neutrality to those expected from object orientation.

The myriads of platform dependencies have been the bane of every development team that faces the challenge of developing a single application that will run on multiple platforms. The traditional strategy, developing the product first for a single target platform, then porting it to others over time, has been a very expensive proposition. Each port typically requires extensive modification of the original code, which in turn requires continual maintenance of multiple versions of the same product.

Porting traditional programs is expensive, time consuming, and error-prone

Using structured techniques to isolate platform-specific code from system-independent code mitigates this problem a little, but creates new disadvantages. C and C++ programmers, for example, often achieve portability through extensive use of the preprocessor, which reduces code readability and adds to maintenance burdens. Code specific to any given platform can easily get subtly out of synch with the rest; testing for such problems becomes very expensive, when it is not shirked altogether.

The isolation strategy was hard enough to apply when developing traditional text-based applications. It becomes even

GUI-based programs add complexity to the porting problem

harder to apply when applications take advantage of today's popular graphical user interfaces (GUIs). GUI systems are similar in basic philosophy, particularly in their event-driven nature, but there is more than one devil in the details. Two versions of an application may look and feel alike, but the code that drives them is not.

Third parties have created large GUI libraries to address this problem. Because the tradeoffs are complex, these libraries vary widely in range of utility, and in price. Some take the least-common-denominator approach, providing only the functionality common to all supported platforms. Others take a more inclusive approach; these typically support most if not all of one main platform's functionality, then jury-rig the code for other platforms to support that same functionality.

In stark contrast, Java's virtual-machine concept and its tight specification should eliminate the need to write platform-specific code in the first place. A single version of a program should run on a wide range of target systems without any developer intervention at all—at least in theory. It is interesting to note that, when portability problems arose in the first Java implementation, they appeared in the GUI portion of the class libraries.

Gains from Interpretation

Interpretation leads to rapid development

Java's combination of compilation and interpretation in a virtual-machine model benefits developers in yet another way. The language's simplicity allows for very rapid compilation to bytecode format, and its runtime interpreter allows for quick execution of modules as they are developed. In place of the traditional—and traditionally tedious—edit-compile-link-run cycle, Java developers experience much faster turnarounds. The result is a much more interactive development process, one that resembles the Rapid Application Development (RAD) methodology that is gaining such popularity.

Java vs. C/C++

It may be easier to see how Java can improve productivity if we compare and contrast it with the two languages serious developers use most often these days. The "flavor" of Java is familiar to C and C++ programmers. It shares some syntactical and semantical features with them, but there are significant differences we should examine in some detail.

Java shares C and C++ features—only up to a point

OO Purity

C supports only procedural code, and C++ is a kitchen-sink hybrid that supports both procedural and OO programming styles. Java requires programmers to write code in an entirely object-oriented way.

Gone is the procedural "Hello, World" program that was the first one written by every C/C++ programmer:

```
#include <stdio.h>
void main(void)
{
   printf("Hello, World\n");
}
```

Java applications are classes, not simply loose collections of functions. All code must be contained in class definitions, even the "main" routine that provides the entry point into an application.

From the very beginning, Java programmers create classes

```
public class HelloWorld
{
   public static void main (String argv[])
   {
      System.out.println ("Hello, World");
   }
}
```

The Java runtime system will recognize that HelloWorld is not only a class but an application because it has a "method" (operation) with a unique signature: it is "public" and "static," it is named "main," and it expects an array of Strings as its only argument and returns "void," i.e., nothing. The RTS will invoke that "main" routine when the application is started, and the class displays the greeting, not by calling a "library function" as in C, but by invoking a method of the System class.

Applets are also classes:

```
import java.awt.*;
import java.applet.*;
public class HelloWorld extends Applet
{
    public void paint (Graphics g)
    {
        g.drawString("Hello, World",50,25);
    }
}
```

In this example, the HelloWorld class "extends," i.e. inherits behavior from, a class already defined in the system library: "Applet." This event-driven library class provides all the basic behavior we need in any Java applet. Ours only displays a greeting at given coordinates of the applet's window, so we need to write only one method: "paint." Note that our method overrides a default "paint" method that HelloWorld inherited from the Applet class.

Classes are the simpler solution... when the problem is complex

Those with little exposure to OO programming often find it hard to believe that creating new classes is simpler than writing C functions. When the first examples they see resemble the ones above, it is easy to understand the reaction: "This is *simpler?*" As examples grow larger and more complex, however, the conviction grows ever firmer that bundling data and operations into independent, self-contained classes is truly much less complicated than constructing elaborate hierarchies of functions.

The hybrid nature of C++ makes it all too easy for programmers to write procedural code instead of taking advantage of the power the language's object-oriented features would give them. A tendency to backslide into these old, familiar programming habits is a major reason that many C++ projects have not delivered the productivity gains that developers hoped for, indeed that motivated the switch to C++ in the first place.

Java's exclusion of syntax that supports procedural programming forces programmers to embrace the OO paradigm completely—and constitutes a principal reason Java is so much simpler than C++.

No Preprocessor

The C/C++ preprocessor is not a true compiler, but rather an elaborate set of translation phases that occur in a separate step, taken before the compiler proper ever sees the code. It uses conditional compilation to conceal platform-dependent code in portable source code, header-file inclusion to enable programmers to centralize declarations of data structures and operations, and text substitution to replace "magic numbers" with symbolic constants and to create small, function-like, in-line routines called macros.

Because the preprocessor operates by substituting text, it cannot know and does not care about such desirable language features as type safety. It is also a major contributor to the complication and illegibility of much of the body of C/C++ code. Java has completely forsaken its use. Java does not need some of the C/C++ preprocessor's services, and has incorporated the genuinely useful ones into the compiler itself.

The preprocessor is a black hole for type safety

The Java compiler is smart enough to delete statically determinable "dead code," and conditional compilation is unnecessary because the language is inherently portable.

Java does not need header-file inclusion because Java programmers do not need header files. In order for C++

No more header files

developers to use a programmer-defined class, they must include a header file at compile time and specify the corresponding library file at link time. In Java, by contrast, each class definition is fully specified in a single file, and a multi-pass compiler searches out class specifications as needed. The programmer lists classes that will be used but does not need to include detailed declarations of them, as in C++. The Java runtime system can find in the bytecode forms of the class files all the information it needs to interpret a program, or to perform JIT compilation.

C/C++ programmers use macros that rely on text substitution to create efficient substitutes for magic numbers, and to define small chunks of code for in-line execution. Macro substitution often achieves runtime efficiency at the cost of "code bloat." Java achieves similar efficiency with less effort on the programmer's part by supplying new type attributes and by simplifying the language in ways that enable a Java compiler to optimize code far more aggressively.

No Operator Overloading

Operator overloading is useful but many C++ programmers overdo it

C++ programmers can define new behavior for existing operators. Used with restraint, operator overloading can simplify syntax for the users of classes they define. Few will argue that overloading is appropriate in complex mathematical code, and in string handling. In almost all other cases, however, it makes code more complex, and reduces rather than enhances legibility and maintainability. Its addition to C++ has made the language much more complicated, yet has added only modest value.

Despite these costs, a strange obsession seems to overtake many C++ programmers. Once they have grasped the basics of the language, they seem to find operator overloading so irresistible that they employ it when it is wildly inappropriate—even go so far as to recast a problem for no other purpose than to force the use of overloaded operators in the solution.

Java's developers concluded that support for programmer-defined operator overloading would complicate the language, open a Pandora's box of potential abuse, and produce little extra value. They chose not to support overloading, with one exception: they saw clear benefits from operator-invoked string handling and little difficulty in integrating it into the language, so they included a String class in the language definition, and overloaded operators for it appropriately.

No goto Statement

C's creator himself disparaged the goto statement as "infinitely abusable," and it is almost universally detested by those who can remember unraveling strands of the "spaghetti code" that was all too easy to write before languages had better loop and branch constructs. Some companies' programming standards forbid its use entirely. Others' allow it only when an exceptional condition requires an abrupt branch out of nested control structures, one that cannot be accomplished by a break or continue statement (which operate only in respect of the innermost structure).

Where a goto would be useful, Java provides a less treacherous alternative

Java's creators acknowledged the occasional need for such a branch, but rejected the raw goto statement as a bit too flexible. Their compromise was to allow labeling of loops and switches, and to allow break and continue statements to refer to labeled statements and thereby ignore nesting.

No Global Variables

Global variables have been described as "the goto of data structures;" right-thinking programmers avoid them whenever they can. Their broad visibility makes them subject to alteration by any part of the program and thus constitutes another source of subtle programming errors that sap productivity.

Java encapsulates all *data*

In Java, as in any other pure OO language, a datum may be defined only within the confines of a class, and is accessible only to code that is part of the same class. Thus severely limiting the datum's scope makes it vastly easier to trace down any error related to it.

No Explicit Pointers

Raw pointers are variables that hold the addresses of other variables. In C and C++ they are a necessary evil, often the only means available to accomplish a desired result, such as construction of a linked list. They represent a notorious source of bugs. Since C and C++ support implicit pointer casting, the compiler cannot know for certain the type of every datum, and as a result cannot optimize code aggressively.

Unhampered by this kind of ignorance, strongly typed languages like Modula-2 often have blazingly fast compilers, and these often produce code that is significantly faster than equivalent C/C++.

Java's type-safe references eliminate whole categories of errors

To simplify some syntax, C++ added "references" to the pointers it inherited from C, but these references are no more type-safe than pointers. Java *replaced* pointers with references that are much more powerful than those found in C++.

A Java reference is a strongly-typed key that provides access to objects of the specified type. The programmer can attach a reference to a class or an interface, but not to a built-in type, and may request only very limited forms of casting. Many uses of references are verified at compile time and the rest are checked at run time.

Replacing clumsy pointer-related syntax with the cleaner syntax of direct references enhances code legibility, and replacing dangerous, uncheckable pointers with type-safe references eliminates a whole class of errors, whose tracing and resolution chew up programmer time that could be better spent developing new products.

No Structures, No Unions

In C and C++ a "structure" is an aggregation of data of disparate types in a single logical construct. A "union" contains only one datum at any one time, but the type of that datum varies. To contrast them simply, a structure can hold "this and that;" a union can hold "this *or* that."

Structures and unions are just degenerate forms of classes

Structures are a useful tool for data abstraction, but the "classes" characteristic of OO languages accomplish the same results and much more.

C++ supports classes, but retains structures for backward compatibility with C. Java eschews structures, for the same reason it does not support global variables or functions: eliminating traditional code and data constructs forces programmers to adhere to the OO paradigm, and thus fosters consistency and simplicity.

The "untyped unions" of C/C++ are dangerous ways to outwit the type system and have no Java equivalent. The "typed unions" found in the Pascal family of languages provide a way to generalize and specialize data types, but Java's inheritance syntax provides a much more elegant way to accomplish the same objectives.

Unicode Character Support

Most implementations of C and C++ specify an eight-bit size for the built-in character type, then provide very limited support for larger character sizes via multi-byte and wide-character library routines.

Java is the first language of note to specify 16-bit Unicode as its basic character type. Unicode can be a major benefit to developers who intend to distribute their software internationally, because it supports their efforts to offer versions in languages that add diacritical marks to Roman characters, e.g., Czech and Swedish, or use a different character set altogether, e.g., Russian and Thai.

Java's Unicode support lays a foundation for unified global communications

Alas, at this writing at least, much of the support for multi-lingual software is still missing, including the complex input systems needed to read Kanji characters (for example). Fonts and display graphics systems are still inadequate as well. Java's fundamental support of Unicode will make it easy to eliminate these shortcomings in the near future.

Java provides a "byte" type for the rare occasions that its 16-bit replacement of the "char" type is undesirable; for example, when a programmer needs to do eight-bit arithmetic.

Boolean Type

Unlike C/C++, Java does not treat true/false values as numeric expressions

Because C and C++ use simple integers to represent true/false values, programmers are free to use numeric expressions in Boolean contexts, and Boolean expressions in numeric contexts. This interchangeability leads to a kind of shorthand that novices must learn to read. It does not take them long to see that "if(x)..." means "if x is not zero..." but overuse of such shortcuts makes code hard to read. A more important downside to the lack of a separate Boolean data type is that it creates yet another area of uncertainty, making it still more difficult for C/C++ compilers to optimize code as thoroughly as they otherwise might.

Java provides a separate type, "boolean," for true/false expressions. All of the conditional operators yield boolean values and all of the conditional statements require boolean test expressions. Boolean variables will not accept any value other than "true" or "false," and default to the latter.

Some C/C++ programmers will miss the compactness of their familiar shorthand, but the elimination of another "typeless hole" should, on balance, increase their productivity.

First-Class Arrays

Arrays provide a convenient way for programmers to store homogeneous values, and few languages lack support for them.

In C/C++, array notation is merely syntactic sugar; the compiler treats array names as pointers and uses pointer arithmetic to perform indexing—and all those pointer problems come back to haunt us once more. Because the compiler cannot compare indexing expressions to array bounds, a program can read or write past the end of the array if the programmer does not spend time building in bounds checks. Weak typing leaves the compiler uncertain as to the actual type of any array element, and thus limits prospects for optimization.

Java replaces syntactic sugar with a true array type

Without pointers to underpin implementation, how does Java support arrays? The language's developers started from scratch, and made arrays first-class citizens of the language itself. From the outside, arrays look like class objects, but array-specific syntax makes it easy for programmers to define arrays, access them, and pass them as parameters.

In Java, arrays are intelligent: they know the sizes of their elements and their own length, and check the validity of access attempts. By obviating the need to write extra code to check indices against bounds, and by eliminating yet another common source of bugs, intelligent arrays lift burdens from the shoulders of programmers, and free them to apply their own intelligence to more worthwhile tasks.

Multiple Inheritance

Enthusiasts claim that object orientation can increase productivity tenfold, and point to inheritance as the most obvious way to achieve such gains. Centralizing specifications for the behavior that a group of related classes share facilitates consistency of interface, yet allows programmers to extend and specialize classes easily. Allowing "subclasses"

C++ confuses two kinds of inheritance

to inherit implementation as well as interface from "super-classes" permits programmers to reuse code on a massive scale.

Taken separately, both "sub-typing" (inheritance of interface) and code reuse (inheritance of implementation) boost productivity—as long as programmers are able to specify whether they want one of these, the other, or both. Unfortunately, C++ does not distinguish between these two forms of inheritance; it gives programmers no convenient syntax to inherit interface without implementation, or implementation without interface.

This rigidity is a nuisance when programmers want to derive a new class from only one superclass—single inheritance, but becomes a major obstacle when they want to inherit behavior of more than one superclass—multiple inheritance. The inability to separate the two kinds of inheritance has made C++ much more complex than it ought to be, and also adds productivity-killing complications to the programmer's job as well. For one thing, it aggravates the "fragile superclass" problem: the need to recompile every class that inherits from one's class after even the most modest change in it.

Java lets programmers inherit interface and implementation separately

Java, on the other hand, provides syntax that allows programmers to inherit interface and implementation separately. The language furnishes similar but distinctive syntax for defining "interfaces" as opposed to fully implemented classes, and allows a new class to support multiple interfaces. This arrangement maps neatly to the most common use of multiple inheritance: getting a single class to exhibit all of the behavior of two or more classes.

From the class user's perspective, consistency of interface is the only important issue; implementation is someone else's job. That "someone else," the class programmer, might be dismayed at first to learn that Java does not support multiple inheritance of implementation—but typically finds that combining object composition with single inheritance accomplishes the same results easily.

The Sather language has demonstrated that, once implementation and interface are clearly distinguished, it is relatively simple to support multiple inheritance of both and still avoid the complications found in C++. Alas, even Java is not perfect.

The differences between C/C++ and Java would fill a book—and indeed books now on the shelves demonstrate that they have. The list above is intended only to summarize differences that have the biggest impact on productivity.

Tools

The first tools Sun supplied to Java developers were clearly a proof-of-concept rather than an attempt to deliver a product of commercial quality. Subsequent tools from Sun and third parties become more impressive and mature with each new version. Because high-quality development tools are critical to productivity, an entire chapter examines their potential (see Chapter 10).

Good work requires good tools

Class Libraries

A rich and varied library of classes is a crucial element of the OO vision. Developers will experience the order-of-magnitude productivity gains promised by OO prophets only when they can pull most of the program components they need "off the shelf."

It is impossible to create so rich a resource overnight. To achieve high levels of code reuse, development groups will need to develop their own business-specific classes, in addition to acquiring classes from the vendors of their primary development tools, and from other third parties.

Developers must develop their own library classes, and acquire others

The range of classes available today is only the beginning of what is likely to be a huge market. A quick look at the size of the Microsoft VXB and OCX markets indicates how much potential there is for third parties to produce libraries and applets that meet the needs of other developers.

The explosion of commercial activity over the Internet is characterized by a similar explosion of cottage industries. Low costs for marketing, sales, and distribution reduce barriers that once blocked entry into the market by small and innovative enterprises. Because small software components lend themselves most readily to 'net distribution, it is reasonable to expect that small, independent developers will carve out a substantial share of the market for Java class libraries and applets. If they make their fortunes at all, it will only be by providing products that make their customers more productive.

Rapid Application Development

For a radical increase in development speed...

Rapid Application Development, RAD, has become one of today's hottest buzzwords. By extending the OOPS concept to a visually oriented design stage, RAD systems allow developers to put applications together quickly, slashing both development times and the costs associated with creating software systems.

Programmers can construct entire applications largely by dragging active components (objects) from a library resource and dropping them onto a work area. This process realizes the long-promised OO goal of snapping together applications out of the software equivalents of Lego blocks. RAD is inherently an interactive process. To be worthwhile, a RAD system must use a language that compiles and links quickly. Its utility would drop to zero if each small change required the programmer to wait 15 minutes while the RAD system rebuilt the application.

Quick turnaround was almost certainly the reason Borland chose its own Turbo Pascal rather than C++ as the language for its Delphi RAD environment. Turbo Pascal is object-ori-

CHAPTER 7 • PRODUCTIVITY

ented and highly modular, and compiles and links very quickly—attributes that make it ideal for a RAD system.

Java shares all of these features, and offers many more that Turbo Pascal does not, including portability, intrinsic multi-threading, synchronization, and security. Used in the code-generation component of a RAD system, Java could combine the speed of drag-and-drop programming with the other productivity gains we have described, and enable a development team to penetrate a wide variety of markets with efficient, secure, reliable products very quickly and maintain them more easily.

Java is a natural for RAD systems

Changes to the SDLC

Java's many productivity-enhancing features will most certainly have an effect on the software development life-cycle. Skilled Java developers drawing on ever richer class libraries should dramatically reduce the time and cost of writing, testing, and debugging.

The highly modular decomposition achievable in Java projects, the very clean interface between objects, and the absence of dangerous language constructs like global variables should enable even quite large teams to develop major projects much more easily, and with much lower risks.

Large-scale encapsulation decreases both costs and risks

That objects are dynamically linked makes it much easier to manage a project of any scale; access to the source code for a superclass is seldom necessary and recompilation of sub-classes can often be avoided even when a superclass is modified. Because programmers need access only to code they work on directly and there are no separate header files, the burdens of code ownership and version control are also significantly reduced.

Java's built-in enforcement of object-oriented design methods should produce systems that are far more modular; components should have far fewer undesired interdependencies. Because objects narrow the scope of data and code, teams can undertake major modifications on some components with little risk of compromising the integrity of others.

Productivity gains may be highest where the burdens are heaviest

Modularity at every level of abstraction should have a particularly large impact on maintenance costs. Functional upgrades are likely to be much simpler, and the simplicity of Java's design and the code validation done by the runtime system can eliminate many of the hard-to-find bugs that tend to bedevil large systems.

Shortening the implementation, testing, and maintenance stages of the SDLC allows more time for the usually short-changed analysis and design stages. The rewards will come in the form, not only of reduced costs, but also of systems that are more reliable, more flexible, and better matched to their users' needs.

The ability to move an entire software system to a new platform without even recompiling it will provide further long-term dividends.

Making the Transition

Once a development organization has made a decision to adopt the Java programming language, the task becomes one of organizing a transition that will impose the lowest possible costs and will least disrupt current work flows. Just as the language decision itself depends on the needs and style of the organization, outside advice on the best approach to the transition must be adapted to fit local concerns.

Wade in the shallows or plunge into the deep end?

Many IS managers or project leaders use the next major software project as a springboard into a new language. Moving so boldly is usually a big mistake. Without prior experience it is very difficult to produce accurate schedules and cost estimates. Unrealistic deadlines increase pressures on programmers already struggling with new tools and a new language. A better approach is to train a small team of two to six talented programmers, and assign them a more modest project.

Some experts recommend that the project objective be a small class library. Library building will be a major part of long-term development in any case, and provides the foundation on which to build all other projects. Even if the pilot library must later be completely rewritten, as it often must, the team gains valuable experience in a fundamental area of OO development.

Other experts argue that the team will need to acquire a feel for producing solutions to actual problems before it can realistically be expected to produce even a good prototype of a reusable class library. They recommend that the pilot team develop a narrowly defined but complete product.

Even before the pilot project, it is vital that the team members receive professional training in object-oriented concepts and techniques generally, and Java specifically. It is a mistake simply to leave them to their own devices unless they already have a very strong grounding in object-oriented design. In the long run, experience is the best teacher, but early on it has a tendency to instill bad habits that are hard to break. An investment in high quality conceptual and practical training will most certainly pay dividends. It is often beneficial to hire or contract a Java expert to help kickstart a project and provide mentoring.

Training and guidance are essential

Once the pilot project is complete, and its results have been evaluated, the members of the pilot team can serve as a nucleus of experts for the larger team that will undertake the next, more ambitious project.

In this chapter, we have seen that the nature of Java enables it to enhance productivity in many ways:

❖ Java supports all of the core OO concepts, with unusually strong potential for increased code reuse, robustness, and flexibility—all of which decrease development, testing, and maintenance time.

Java enhances productivity in a dozen ways

- Java's architecture neutrality opens up a much wider marketplace with much less development effort than traditional languages.

- Java's interpreted nature aids portability and rapid development of systems.

- Java does away with the dangerous complexities of C++; a cleaner, simpler language is much faster to learn and much easier to use.

- Java's intrinsic support for Unicode gives it a big head start in furnishing programs with multi-lingual capability.

- Java's modularity and portability make it attractive to toolmakers, whose products have begun a rapid rise from immaturity to richly varied capability.

8

Security

Java-capable Web browsers download applets to local systems so easily that often we are not even aware of the process. Such automated program distribution is refreshingly conve-nient, but is it safe? What if the applet is malicious, and will attempt to destroy valuable data? What if a virus has infected it? What if it is designed to copy sensitive data through the Internet to some unknown location?

Until we have satisfying answers to these questions about risks and security, we cannot be comfortable surfing the Web with a Java-driven browser. In this chapter we assess the risks entailed by downloading executable code, and investi-gate the security features built into Java that help us manage those risks.

The Risks

The threats to our systems' security we describe are so com-mon that they have been given names: Trojan Horses, viruses, snoopers, and sniffers.

**Figure 8.1
Potential perils of
perusing public applets**

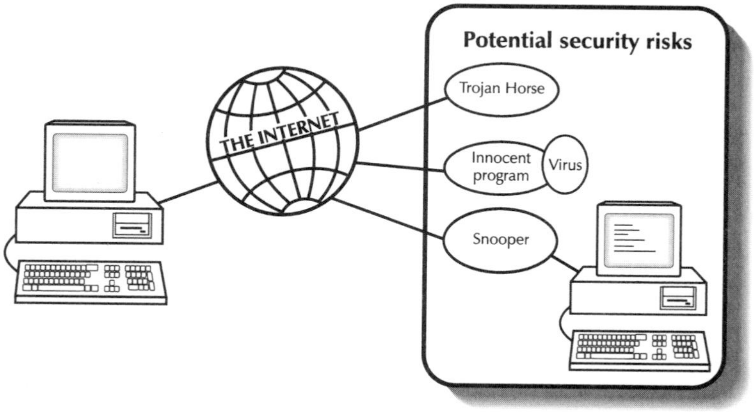

Trojan Horses

*Beware strangers
bearing gifts*

Trojan Horse programs call to mind their ancient namesake
by hiding malicious intent behind a benign facade. Uncover-
ing their attempts to subvert systems is particularly hard
when they conceal themselves in, or disguise themselves as,
legitimate programs. They typically find their way into a system when its administrator installs what appears to be—but
is not—a new version of genuine software.

The canonical example envelops or entirely replaces the
standard password program. It looks and acts like the real
thing—but it also sends account names and passwords to
the "cracker" who deployed it. The objective of this Trojan
Horse and many others is not usually to wreak havoc at the
moment, but rather to facilitate later access by viruses and
spies.

Viruses

*The only safe form of
network computing is
abstinence*

Virus programs are especially insidious because they propa-
gate themselves. They most closely resemble their biological
analogues in systems with little or no built-in security, e.g.,
PCs running Windows and Macintosh computers: in such
"unprotected" systems, they attach themselves like parasites
to legitimate programs. In UNIX and similar systems, viruses

tend to be combinations of programs that exploit flaws all too common in system programs like sendmail and the shell.

When an infected program is run, the virus activates and usually tries to replicate itself for a while. It often cheekily announces its presence just before it does something relatively harmless like corrupting the current display, or horribly destructive like reformatting a disk.

Snoopers and Sniffers

Some spy programs do not actually invade a system, but rather sit on the outside and "snoop" or "sniff" at data flows, looking for valuable information they can copy for later use. The distinction between snoopers and sniffers is subtle enough that we can leave it to security experts; the important fact is that both are rife on the Internet.

Snoopers and sniffers troll for data on the 'net

Recall that the 'net is a huge network of systems connected by a web of communications links, and that any given communication on the 'net may pass through a dozen systems before reaching its destination. A sniffer may be sitting on any link, scanning each packet of data that goes by, for account names and passwords let us say. When it finds them, it forwards them to its creator, who will then have the means to gain access to a computer targeted for nefarious purposes.

Java's Built-in Safeguards

Do we allow complete strangers unlimited access to our homes? Of course not. We put up fences with gates, and install locks on doors. Java provides a number of mechanisms to ensure we can create, manage, and use stranger applets safely. These include one level of security provided by the language itself, two furnished by the Java Virtual Machine, and more.

Java builds fences and installs locks to protect our valuables

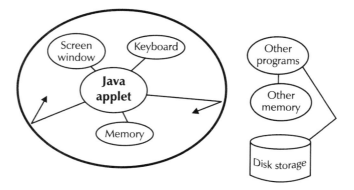

Figure 8.2
An applet isolated by Java's built-in security features

Language Safety

The language itself provides the first-level security mechanism. As is detailed in Chapter 7, Java's designers placed a high priority on security. They simply excluded language features that are notoriously insecure, or severely restricted them to a manageable form. They replaced raw pointers with "type-safe references," and cleaned up the typing system generally.

Elimination of these potential security holes was important in itself, but it has another benefit: it results in a kind of predictability that enables vendors to create flexible higher level mechanisms, and policies that allow selection of security features appropriate to a particular environment.

Protection Provided by the Virtual Machine

Traditional compiled languages offer little, if any, language-level security

The Java Virtual Machine provides two levels of security that are unattainable when we use traditional fully compiled languages like Pascal and C++.

If the executable form of program contains instructions that the computer's processor executes directly, it has the potential to exploit weaknesses in the operating system. It may deliberately compromise the system's integrity, or gain access to sensitive information.

A Java executable, by contrast, is never in this position. It is not executed directly by the processor, but rather by an implementation of the VM, which is therefore in an excellent position to maintain complete control over the actions of every Java program. Its "verifier" and "class loader" components perform second- and third-level security operations, respectively.

Whenever the Java runtime system loads a program, its Bytecode Verifier performs a number of security checks:

Bytecode verification guarantees Java programs are well formed—and more

1   File-format validation. The verifier rejects any file that does not fit the distinctive format of Java bytecode files, thereby averting accidental execution of what might appear to be valid instructions but are not.

2   Bytecode validation. It then closely scrutinizes the bytecode that makes up the program for errors in construction.

3   Data-flow validation. It then searches for potential runtime errors such as stack overflow.

The program cannot execute until these checks are complete; verification thus eliminates many common problems before they arise. Load-time testing also improves overall execution speed: it is more efficient to perform a given test once, when the program is loaded, than to repeat it every time the interpreter encounters an instruction it may execute thousands of times.

An ounce of prevention is worth a pound of cure

The verifier ensures that a program's bytecode adheres to the statically determinable semantics of the language. There is no need to trust that a compiler on some foreign system has produced safe code, because the verifier runs on the client side of the link. This unique security feature, among others, gives Java a big edge over competitors like ActiveX and Inferno/Dis.

But "who guards the guardian?" What if someone has tampered with the verifier itself? That risk is no greater than the one we run when we buy any software distributed through normal commercial channels. Viruses seldom arrive in shrink-wrapped packages from established suppliers. Buying the Java runtime system from a trusted vendor and arranging delivery through a secure medium reduces the risk to a level we are obliged to accept every day.

The class loader separates Java code into isolated spaces

Once the verifier has completed its checks, it hands the program over to the "class loader." This component of the Java runtime system isolates Java classes in separate, inviolate areas. It segregates each class from all others, but it also isolates categories of classes from each other in security domains—"built-in classes" that are part of the Java run time; "local classes" that have been installed in one's own account; "foreign classes" that come from the outside world.

Separating built-in classes from local classes, and foreign classes from both, enables the Java run time to prevent ill-intentioned code from "spoofing" the system—in this case, by duping it into using a spurious class from an unknown source in place of a built-in class.

System-Access Restrictions on Applets

Java allows different policies to suit differing needs and uses

The first three levels of Java security provide a foundation upon which we can build higher levels of security. The Java VM runtime system provides "hooks" that let us decide what higher level security policies are appropriate for any given product. We may specify quite different policies for a Java application running in a local environment, a Java applet running in the same environment, and an applet running in a foreign environment.

Java-enabled browsers are likely to have the most complex security policies because they run code from a variety of sources. Code built into the browser is trusted implicitly. Code from a local source is often given relatively free rein, but not necessarily—Netscape's Navigator v2.0 has a more stringent policy than the Appletviewer in Sun's Java Development Kit in this regard.

The Java runtime system imposes harsh constraints upon foreign, "untrusted" applets. It may prohibit them from manipulating local files at all, or limit their access to an isolated directory created by the class loader. It also controls their ability to create and use network connections, usually restricting them to communications with the host from which they were downloaded. The user interface earmarks all new windows created by an untrusted applet, to prevent it from representing itself as a trusted applet.

Foreign applets are regarded with extreme prejudice

A typical Java runtime system provides underlying mechanisms that support a wide diversity of security policies—and permits policies to be changed on the fly. Its vendor may build in access-control lists and heuristic rule sets, and system-configuration screens typically allow users to specify their preferences.

Java security is dynamic and modifiable

These measures provide a very high level of protection against the dangers of downloading and running untrusted applets. It becomes exceedingly difficult for anyone to create an insecure applet and actually get it to run on a client's system.

Can Applets Still Be Useful?

Are Java's security features so stringent that they render applets useless? Not at all. Applets were always intended to serve limited purposes in any case. Even without access to the computer's file system, or the ability to open connections to other computers, they can perform simple but highly useful tasks.

Foreign applets are useful even within tough security constraints

We describe several examples in Chapter 4, but one application area critical to corporate information systems staff is worth mentioning here: database access and manipulation. Scores of companies are developing the support and tools needed to facilitate use of Java programs in each of the roles possible in two- and three-tier client-server systems: applications with direct DB connectivity; applications or trusted applets as application-level servers; applets as thin or thick clients.

Java meets the security needs of corporate "intranets" as well as the global Internet

It is important to remember that it is the Internet's anarchic, open-ended nature that obliges us to rely on applets whose source may be dubious, and therefore to develop rigorous security policies as a defense.

On LANs and most WANs, by contrast, a single organization owns the network, defines its limits explicitly, and can manage its content much more precisely. A corporation can establish an intranet, an enterprise-wide network that takes advantage of the flexibility of Internet technology yet remains closed-ended and carefully controlled. In an intranet, the organization can rely much less on completely foreign, untrusted Java applets, and much more on "enterprise-wide applets" it deploys only after careful screening. These may be developed internally, or acquired from trusted external suppliers through secure means.

With greater confidence that the applets themselves are benign, the organization can afford more relaxed constraints on their operation. Java's higher-level security features give the Java runtime system the option to tighten limits on file-system access, network connections, and so on, but they also give it the option to loosen them. On a locally controlled intranet, surrendering some control of the machine to an applet is no longer equivalent to surrendering control entirely.

Design Considerations

Perfect security is a myth

No matter how well designed a security system is, it cannot guarantee that it has absolutely no weak points. No one should be complacent about the levels of protection provided by *any* security system, Java included.

Any computer system that is connected to the Internet either full time or on a transient basis should be designed, implemented, and administered in ways that ensure levels of security, privacy, protection, and simplicity appropriate to its uses. Good network management, regular virus checking, firewalls, and other common-sense barriers to security and integrity breaches are essential. Even when they cannot completely prevent a problem arising, they may well limit its scope.

The morbidly pessimistic will say that security and the Internet will always be mutually exclusive. Incurable optimists will dismiss security concerns far too lightly. A prudent, common-sense approach to security is best.

Those concerned about the risks Java applets may pose to the security and integrity of their operations should first take a brief look at other potential weaknesses in their defenses.

Security is like a balloon: one tiny hole...

How easy would it be for an employee to copy valuable data from the system to a floppy disk and carry it out in a shirt-pocket? What would it cost to prevent such theft? There are too many well documented cases of disgruntled former employees laying waste to their employers' systems before they left, or planting delayed-action Trojan Horses which later caused chaos. Organizations can eliminate or greatly reduce many of these risks by using the security mechanisms built into most network operating systems.

System administrators should consult security experts, and should periodically ask themselves the key questions: Do we have appropriate system-level security? Do we conduct periodic audits of our security policies and mechanisms? Are all of the users selecting good passwords, and changing them often? Do we make and test backups regularly?

Security is a concern that never goes away

The design of the Java applet system is extremely secure and well thought out. The security of any computer system is only as strong as the weakest link, but in most installations

Java is highly unlikely to be that weak link. None of the security violations seen so far resulted from design flaws. All were caused by bugs in the implementation of the system, and all were fixed promptly.

The general consensus among security experts who have examined Java's security mechanisms is that they are first-rate.

9

Protection of Intellectual Property Rights

Sun's Rights

 As its creator, Sun Microsystems has been very careful to protect its rights in the valuable intellectual property that is Java. On Sun's Web site, several pages explain the terms and conditions it imposes on developers, and indicate a strong determination to exercise its rights to combat any infringement of the trademarks it has registered for the Java name and logo.

Sun has gone to great lengths to protect "Java" and other trademarks

Product names incorporating any of Sun's trademarks are not recommended; calling a product "Turbo-Java" would be an open invitation to a visit by Sun's lawyers at the very least. A developer may mention the fact that its product is written in Java, but only under specified terms and conditions. To develop the product at all the manufacturer must comply with all terms of the Sun Java license.

The reason for Sun's seemingly draconian attitude toward infringement of its trademarks is quite simple. If a trademark's owner fails to control the trademark and police infringements of it, it will soon be regarded as a generic term, as happened with "nylon." Once a trademark falls into common usage, and is considered to be generic, it no longer enjoys the protection of trademark law. Sun will defend the Java name and logo just

> ### Disclaimer
> *This chapter is intended as a broad overview of legal questions in lay terms, not as definitive interpretation of the law. For authoritative legal advice, the reader will of course want to seek professional counsel.*

as Coca-Cola actively discourages use of "Coke" without the capital C, and for the same reason: to protect their investment of large sums to develop brand awareness.

Sun may have learned a lesson from Microsoft's experience with the name "Windows." Microsoft was able to register its Windows logo as a trademark, but by the time it submitted an application concerning the name, "windows" had already become a generic term within the computer industry. Now any developer can use 'Windows' in the name of its product, an outcome Sun does not want to duplicate with Java.

Sun controls some things more tightly than others

Sun does not unreasonably withhold use of most of its trademarks as long as an intending user registers with the company and agrees to terms and conditions. The only exceptions are the official Java Coffee Cup and Duke logos. Sun is reserving these for its own use, and would take a dim view of anyone else incorporating either of them into an applet. Refusing to license these logos furnishes Sun absolute protection against trademark loss as a result of common use. Developers may use the "Java Powered" logo and the "Java Compatible" logos to indicate that Java was used to develop their products.

Trademark

A word, name, symbol, or device used by a manufacturer of goods to identify those goods and distinguish them from goods manufactured by others.

Sun has also made it quite clear it will control the language specification itself strictly. One of the terms and conditions imposed on even the largest licensees is that they not modify the language without Sun's express consent. This restriction is essential to preserve Java's platform and implementation independence. If vendors were free to "enhance" the language *ad libitum*, irreparable damage could be done to Java's potential as a mainstream language.

Developers' Rights

When combined, the nature of the Internet and the design of Java pose new problems for developers wanting to establish and protect intellectual property rights in their products.

Some pages on the World Wide Web receive many thousands of visitors each day. Incorporation of a Java applet into a Web page could result in hundreds of thousands of copies of it being distributed all over the globe in a very short time, without any form of direct payment to its developer.

Developers, too, need to understand their rights

Does inclusion of a Java applet into a Web page imply that the developer has released it into the public domain, or does the developer still own the copyright and associated intellectual property rights? What about the way Java is implemented and the potential that it provides for use of others' work without acknowledgment or compensation?

The whole concept of freely distributing applets across the Internet creates a host of potential problems that must be considered by anyone contemplating the use of Java to develop them.

Copyright

In most countries, copyright law states that the creator of a work becomes the holder of its copyright unless that copyright is explicitly assigned by way of contract or agreement. If a work is "made for hire," the employer holds the copyright.

Authorship implicitly creates a copyright

Under current US law, copyright protection arises automatically when an original work of authorship is "fixed."

The copyright owner has the exclusive right to publish the work. The act of publishing a work does not invalidate the copyright holder's rights in respect to ownership and entitlements. The publishing medium is not the controlling factor; for example, publishing a book on the Web does not put the work in the public domain, and thus invalidate the copyright, any more than publishing a work in traditional book form does. Regardless of the number of individual copies distributed, or that they were published through the Internet, Java applets remain the intellectual property of their developer.

> ### *Copyright*
> The exclusive right granted to the author of original, fixed works to reproduce, modify, distribute, publicly perform, and publicly display the author's works.

Rights regarding applets are analogous to those regarding the HTML code used to create Web pages. Each time the page or applet is accessed, a copy of that code is sent from the Web server to the viewer's own computer. Since this copying process is essential for the operation of the Web, it must be accepted that, as with HTML code, any Java applet developed for use on the Internet is freely distributed.

The publication medium is not the crucial issue

Do applet developers need copyright protection for their applets? The answer is an unequivocal "yes." The act of accessing a Web page containing a Java applet does not permanently install that applet on the user's system, but any competent programmer can devise mechanisms to capture the downloaded components and save them to disk. A pirate can thus steal applet code and use it for purposes other than those of the site from which it was obtained.

If a competitor can derive significant benefit from unauthorized use of an applet obtained in this way, it makes sense for the original developer to make full use of copyright law and other means to protect the developer's individual property.

Some applets need more protection than others

This kind of abuse is less likely than it might appear at first, however. Typically, a Java applet is only a small component of a larger system, providing some client-side functionality that is useless without the matching server-side programs. If these are secure on the server, there is little value in stealing the applet. To obtain any benefit, a pirate would need to develop duplicates of the server programs, in addition to reverse-engineering the applet to ensure correct interface between them. The effort entailed is likely to be prohibitive.

Protecting Applets by Legal Means

If an applet does need copyright protection, the simplest and most obvious means is to include a copyright notice, preferably one that remains visible the entire time the applet is running. Such a notice is not a requirement for obtaining or protecting a copyright, but it is a good idea: it effectively removes any potential for misunderstanding about ownership—and it may deter copying.

Copyright notices are not obligatory, but they help

A similar method provides equal protection—incorporating a visible registered trademark into the applet. Obtaining a federal trademark is relatively expensive, however. Registering the copyright is much cheaper (about $20) and easier (simple form, no lawyer needed)—and if done in a timely manner entitles the copyright holder to statutory damages in any infringement suit.

Both mechanisms provide the full protection of the law and allow for recovery of actual and punitive damages. The cost of defending an infringement action may by itself be enough to deter unauthorized use or redistribution of applet code.

Protecting Applets by Technical Means

Developers can also apply programming solutions to the problem of guarding an applet against theft, such as a built-in electronic-key algorithm that requires a matching key on the server. Without the matching key, a pirate would have to take time to reverse-engineer the applet to make it work at all. Even a small amount of time is likely to be costly enough to wipe out the benefit of stealing the applet rather than creating a new one from scratch.

Legal techniques are not the only kind of defense developers can deploy

It is possible to limit an applet to communication with its developer's server rather than the server from which it was downloaded. Building in this kind of protection is fairly simple, but breaching it is not a major undertaking either. It should be seen as at best a minor deterrent.

Given that applets are inherently small and simple programs, it is seldom worthwhile to devote significant amounts of time and effort to building in protection at the programming level. Indeed, overzealous use of such mechanisms can degrade performance and reliability.

At present, developers can deploy a number of strategies in combination, each of them intended to add a layer of frustration for would-be pirates, but the inherent uselessness of many applets when they are isolated from their servers is likely to be their best single protection against theft.

"Trusted-applet" technology may enable developers to "broadcast" applets, yet still control their use

"Trusted applets" may soon provide a much more promising line of approach. Such applets are called "trusted" because they provide a mechanism by which users of an applet can assure themselves that it came from a trusted source. Once the necessary encryption technology is in place, however, it can be used to establish trust in the opposite direction as well. A developer will be able to publish an applet openly yet ensure that only customers who have purchased licenses are able to use it. After exchanging keys with the developer, legitimate users will be able to download an encrypted applet and decrypt it; others will be able to download it but will not have the key necessary to convert it back to a usable form.

Capitalizing on Applet Redistribution

"It is better to give than to receive" ...and than to retain, sometimes

Rather than obsess over losses that might result from the theft of applets, developers might be wiser to focus on gains that might be had from using free distribution of applets as a sales and marketing tool. Most businesses are happy to have their Web pages accessible through the Internet because the information they contain boosts sales of their products and services. Well-designed Java applets have a similar potential.

A growing number of pages on the Web feature Java applets that do little more than promote a company's products or services. A freely distributed applet that conveys a message in a unique, innovative, or entertaining manner can be an excellent promotional tool. Animated, interactive applets have far more visual impact than static Web-page images; an outstanding applet cannot help but gain valuable exposure for the message it delivers.

CHAPTER 9 • INTELLECTUAL PROPERTY RIGHTS

A growing number of books provide more in-depth treatment of intellectual property rights in the software industry, among them *Multimedia Law and Business Handbook* by Brinson and Radcliffe, cited in the Bibliography.

Developers need to be clear about Sun's rights, and their own

Java developers need to understand and adhere to the conditions and restrictions Sun places on the use of its Java trademarks, because they can affect the choice of product name, package design, and so forth. Using "Java" in the name would require permission Sun does not appear eager to give—and it will be hard to find a coffee-related name not already trademarked by another developer!

Software developers establish defensible intellectual property rights in their products simply by creating them, whether in Java or in any other modern programming language. They should consider both legal and technical means to protect their rights, but should also consider the benefits that may be gained by allowing free redistribution of specially designed applets through the Internet.

10

Third-Party Support

 The success of any computer language depends, not only on the quality and availability of its implementations, but on the support third parties provide. Java can showcase its features in a variety of representations only if development efforts from many parts of the industry augment Sun's own continuing support.

The role of third-party support in past successes demonstrates its importance. Pascal drowsed for years in academia until Borland thrust it into the world of mainstream applications development in the mid 1980s. Several other mainstream vendors had produced implementations suitable for real-world development, without much impact. True, Borland's product was technically superior, but the key to its success was the emphasis the company placed on marketing the product.

Experience shows that strong developer support can lead to success...

For contrast, consider IBM OS/2's difficulty in gaining share in the PC market. Early OS/2 versions had flaws that enabled Microsoft's Windows to establish a dominant position. Versions 2 and 3 (the latter dubbed Warp) corrected these flaws and brought true 32-bit processing to PCs long before Microsoft's Windows NT and Windows 95 reached the market. Few could disagree with IBM's claim that OS/2 was an entire generation ahead of its competition. Its user base at long last moved past the 10-million mark, yet tens of millions of dollars spent on marketing failed to break Microsoft's grip on the market.

Why have traveling roadshows, television advertising, special offers, preloading, and a host of other sales and marketing tactics failed to achieve success for a superior product?

...and that inadequate support can hurt even a superior product

The simple answer is that IBM made far too little effort to win the support of developers. The company charged developers hundreds of dollars for its C/C++ compiler, libraries, and toolset for OS/2, and hundreds more for an annual subscription to its developer's resource CD-ROM. Failing to find a warm welcome, developers produced comparatively few native-OS/2 applications, and end users saw too few reasons to buy IBM's product. If IBM had spent a mere 10 per cent of its retail marketing budget on recruiting developers, perhaps the Justice Department would be concerning itself with IBM's market dominance rather than Microsoft's.

In the Starring Role of Creator

Sun gave Java a head-start

Sun chose to give a different kind of performance in its role as Java's creator. The company moved a new product with exciting potential out of the lab and into the market, and promoted it well. As a result, Java captured the media limelight and generated unprecedented levels of interest among developers.

History may show that Java's success began with Sun's success in arousing the interest and enthusiasm of the developer community. Some of that enthusiasm can be attributed to Java's inherent appeal to programmers who were frustrated by C's lack of object-oriented features, and by the excessive complication of OO support in C++. As IBM found, however, a better product is not enough. Giving free and easy access to the first Java implementation and continuing to provide services to developers may prove to be the crucial difference.

How can giving away a product help its creator? The answer lies in leverage Java can provide to Sun in its most important market, the exploding Internet community. Sun is already a very large player in this marketplace, commanding a majority share of the Internet-server market. Corporate success depends on finding ways to maintain this lead in the face of competition from such other industry giants as Intel, Microsoft, and SGI.

Sometimes it pays to give the product away

Sun does not intend to earn a significant profit on Java directly. If the company sold rather than gave away its Java tools, the resulting revenues would hardly figure prominently in Sun's annual report. The returns they expect are more indirect and long-term. Sun hopes to turn Java into a key component of the Internet, thereby maintaining the company's high profile and positioning itself to sell many more of its core products. Sun is attempting to maintain and expand market share by creating an innovative technology — an exercise quite different from Microsoft's attempt to move into a market merely by bundling free Internet software into Windows 95.

Sun has been very careful to retain full control over the design of Java, believing that allowing licensees to "enhance" the language would threaten its integrity. Having seen the effects of uncontrolled extensions to other languages, they have reason to worry that similar alterations to the Java specification would erode many of its key benefits. Languages such as C++, whose specifications are drafted by committees, are renowned for their slow pace of evolution, and for incompatibility among various implementations. Sun's tight grip on the language's design, and its retention of the right to decide what is a valid implementation of Java and what is not, should ensure smooth evolution of the language, as well as consistency among all products bearing the Java name.

Sun will continue to decide what is and what is not Java

Of course, we can expect to see "Java-like" products emerge, but they will not be Java and they undoubtedly will find it hard to carve out market share against the strong competition of a widely accepted standard.

Supporting Players

Major supporting actors joined the cast early

A number of large corporations stepped into supporting roles even before the Java curtain went up. Many developed new versions of their existing software or hardware to include support for Java. Others provided even stronger support by developing products specifically for the Java language and environment. The roster of early licensees indicates that Java impressed most of the big names in information technology, including AT&T, Borland, IBM, Microsoft, Netscape, Novell, Oracle, Silicon Graphics, and Symantec. We can illustrate the magnitude of their commitment with a few examples:

Borland

Java is a big part of Borland's return to its strong point, developer tools

After emerging from a period of financial stress and rationalizing its product lines and business resources, Borland signaled its return to its core business by announcing several tools for Java developers. It committed to incorporating facilities for Java development into current C++ development products, and to supplying new tools specifically for Java.

These include several tools for their C++ for Windows IDE: a Java debugger (written in Java), a JIT compiler, and a project manager.

The combination of these tools allows developers to build and mix projects using both C++ and Java. Borland also announced it would support Java with a new version of its Delphi for Windows, a popular rapid application development (RAD) tool suitable for large projects.

CHAPTER 10 • THIRD-PARTY SUPPORT

Symantec

We saw a very early indication that we can expect to see rapid growth in Java tools and environments when Symantec released Version 1.0 of its Café IDE in March 1996, and pre-releases even earlier (see Figure 10.1). This very fast time to market earned Symantec high praise, and no doubt considerable spin-off benefit. Even the first Café was a nicely integrated IDE tailored to production of Java applications and applets. It looked much like Symantec's C/C++ environment, and offered many features missing from the standard Sun JDK. Among the tools included were visual resource builders, project construction facilities, and context-based help/API reference.

Symantec offered a Java IDE very early. Its performance improved

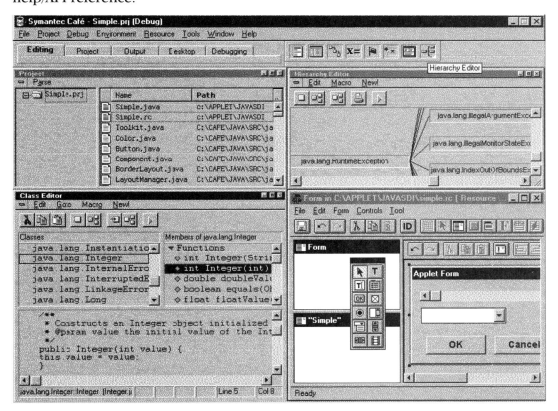

Figure 10.1
An integrated development environment for Java programmers

Symantec also took the first step toward addressing the performance penalties associated with the use of a virtual machine. Its interpreter executes Java bytecode almost twice as fast as the original Sun version, when used on Windows 95 and Windows NT. The company has also supplied a JIT compiler which speeds up Java performance by at least an order of magnitude.

IBM

Java is part of IBM's strategy to penetrate the Internet market

The announcement by IBM that it intended to support Java was just one step in a continuing program of extensive investment in Internet technology. It has created its own Internet service network, the IBM Global Network, and included a suite of Internet applications in OS/2 Warp.

Perhaps the oddest part of IBM's Java announcement was its stated intention to produce a Java implementation for Windows 3.1, when Microsoft itself apparently had no such plans. Such a project appears even more unusual when we consider that Windows 3.1's primitive design, 16-bit architecture, and lack of multi-threading make such an implementation much more complicated than a version for Warp or Windows 95.

The rationale for this seemingly bold step derives from the agreement the two companies signed when Microsoft bowed out of their joint OS/2 development effort. Under the terms of that agreement, IBM retained the right for its "WIN-OS/2" to emulate v.3.1, but not later Windows versions. It may be that IBM's Java for Windows 3.1 will work in WIN-OS/2 but not in MS-Windows.

IBM's Lotus Notes, a cross-platform workgroup system, is exactly the kind of product that can benefit most from Java's network-friendly, architecture-neutral character. Developing all or even part of Notes in Java should make its networking elements easier to implement, and should reduce significantly the burden of maintaining software that must run on many different platforms.

Microsoft

Some analysts believe that Microsoft badly overestimated the amount of cross-marketing power it would derive when it decided to compete against commercial services like America OnLine and Compuserve. Since that time, the software giant has completed an about-face and is now positioning itself as a supplier of Internet technology rather than a competitor to existing online services.

Products from Microsoft support Web users and servers

Microsoft's first Internet product of note was the Internet Explorer, a Web browser which quickly gained a small but significant following. In addition to addressing the client side of the Internet connection, Microsoft put significant muscle behind a push into the server market. The Internet Information Server software for Windows NT strengthens its entry into the market for Internet applications.

Although Microsoft has licensed Java and announced an intention to incorporate Java in its Internet products, some observers suspect that the company is simply taking out a little insurance against the possible failure of its own proprietary offerings. For a long time, Microsoft has fancied itself a leader rather than a follower, and its position on Java only draws attention to that self- perception.

How serious is Microsoft's commitment to Java?

For example, Microsoft competes fiercely against Borland and Symantec in the language market, yet it seems to have no intention to add Java support to any of its language products. Instead, the company prefers to concentrate on its own network-model solutions.

Netscape

As the leading supplier of Web browser software, Netscape has worked closely with Sun to promote the Java applet model from the very beginning. Netscape Navigator has supported applets with a built-in Java interpreter since Release 2.0. This browser's popularity ensured that a large number of users would see the many capabilities of Java applets,

The dominant browser vendor has worked with Sun from the beginning

and thereby fostered the growth in Internet users' acceptance of Java.

Oracle

Oracle and others declare their faith in a consumer-electronics approach to Internet access

Along with several other industry giants, Oracle announced its intention to create "Internet appliances." In concept, an Internet appliance is a simplified computer that limits operations to those with a Web-based interface. The advantages of this type of device to end users lie in its low cost and ease of use.

Advocates of the Internet appliance believe that it will complete the transition of the Internet from a scientific and academic tool to a consumer service. Oracle's chairman was one of the first to espouse the concept, and his belief in its potential that led to Oracle's licensing of Java technology. It was only natural that a supplier of Internet servers and related technology would see Java as an important part of its product offerings.

...and a Cast of Thousands

The Java drama will almost certainly provide roles for thousands of spear-carriers and walk-ons.

Large software companies have bought in or pushed out smaller competitors

Huge software companies dominate the software market. The opportunity for a garage-sized software enterprise to create a successful commercial application all but disappeared years ago. Even many medium-sized development companies have been swallowed up in acquisitions, increasing the trend toward an industry comprising a small number of large players.

One reason for this shift has been the growing complexity of software. Ten years ago an enterprising programmer could write a commercial-quality, full-featured word processor or database program in a few months of weekends and evenings spent at the keyboard. A decade later, giants like

Microsoft spend vast numbers of man-years and millions of dollars developing each application—and invest similar sums in marketing them. How can a small start-up developer hope to compete against firms that can deploy resources on that scale?

We can begin to answer that question by asking another: Where did today's successful software companies start? Often by creating software toolboxes and small utility programs that were in turn used by other developers to create end-user applications. The object-oriented paradigm has long promised to provide a similar but broader path to success that begins in the concept of "software components."

The OO paradigm can enable small companies to become large ones, as in the past

Traditional software systems are rigidly structured, and it is often hard to separate and reuse parts of them that are larger than a low-level subroutine yet smaller than a complete program. A central tenet of OO development, by contrast, is that software must be built out of "objects" of all sizes that are highly self-contained—and reusable. Just as in the auto industry a small manufacturer of bumper guards can succeed by selling its modest products to General Motors, a small software company can succeed by selling software components.

If products are small enough to be developed by a company of any size, individuals and small companies actually have one advantage over large companies: their simpler structures spare them the much greater management costs of large organizations.

"Software components" can help small enterprises overcome their weaknesses and capitalize on their strengths

Given that object-oriented languages have been available for decades, why has this prospect not been realized? One major constraint has been the distribution problem: with their limited resources it has been difficult for small enterprises to reach a large number of users with advertising, let alone with the product itself.

The Internet, and particularly the World Wide Web, provide a communications medium that for the first time puts the small enterprise on an even footing with the industry giant.

Either can put up a Web page for the same modest cost, and there is little reason why more potential customers should visit one page rather than the other.

Java may reduce yet another advantage that larger companies have had—the ability to reach a large market. Profitability often depends on having the largest possible market. Heretofore a principal means to reach a broad market has been to develop a product version for each popular platform, and the same wealth that makes it possible for giants to develop large systems has also put them in a better position to support multiple platforms. If Java is successful, its platform independence will enable a small enterprise to sell the same version of a product to every user in a very large customer base.

Furthermore, the burgeoning Java community itself is a fresh new market, eagerly awaiting the kinds of products that have turned small companies into big ones in the past. Thousands of programmers and software houses are starting to investigate and experiment with Java, and the first thing they discover is a dearth of libraries and toolsets. Even if we take into account the solid opening positions taken by major companies, we still find opportunities for many other players, of every size. Small companies have already created faster interpreters, JIT compilers, and other products for which there is an immediate and very large market.

Adopting these new tools, companies that target the end user have created applications that employ the powerful features of Java. Some of these applications enhance existing ones by adding capabilities not previously available. Other, more revolutionary applications are changing the way end users execute and interact with computing tools.

The nature of applets as small programs of unique functionality also makes them natural products of small innovative companies. As with software components generally, we find that it simply does not take much overhead for a backyard programmer to create a 20KB applet; lower development costs translate to a more attractive price. By lowering the entry barriers, Java opens the gates to a flood of new software.

The advent of any new technology inevitably opens up yet another market: training. The sudden interest in Java immediately created a demand for training that far outstripped the meager supply of experienced Java professionals. As the first trainees become the second generation of trainers, the near absence of qualified trainers will disappear, but as Java grows into a mainstream product, larger numbers of IS managers will see the need to obtain training for development staff.

Like any new technology, Java creates a demand for training

The way Sun handled Java's roll-out got the language off to a flying start. Early support by big names in the industry added momentum. Thousands of individuals and small companies found it easy both to consume and to produce Java programs big and small. And all three parts of this growing cast of characters contribute to Java's rapidly growing base of developer support.

Growth of support for Java started fast and continues to accelerate

11

The Future of Java

It has been said that gazing into the crystal ball of the computer industry is the pastime of fools. That so many rising stars, hailed with high expectations, fade and die should keep seers from being overconfident. In the case of Java, however, a number of predictions can be made with a high degree of certainty.

The popularity of the Internet will undoubtedly continue to rise toward the point at which most computers are connected to each other. Corporations will demand, not only that applications provide ever greater functionality and performance, but that they cooperate with other applications, and that they integrate seamlessly into both the corporate network and the Internet. Quite apart from the contributions it can make to the richness and reliability of conventional applications, Java, with its object orientation, platform independence, and other features, is uniquely suited to the task of making the vision of global integration a reality.

Java supports what the corporate world demands

Some technologies will complement Java and further its growth—and others will provide fierce competition. Whether Java can make good its claim to be the language of tomorrow will depend heavily on the support it gets from the former and on how well it meets the challenges of the latter.

Technologies that Complement

Java will continue to depend on hardware and software from many companies

Tools and technologies of many kinds contribute to the networking model to which Java lends itself so readily. Third-party software has proven to be vital in Java's short past, and will undoubtedly be crucial to its future. Support from hardware devices such as Internet appliances and Java-based microprocessors will be another key factor. Distributed-object computing and other innovative ideas will also strengthen Java as it becomes more widely accepted as a powerful general-purpose programming environment.

Software Tools

Sun has done much to foster the growth of Java, and has also relied on support from major vendors of development tools, server software, and browsers. These third parties will continue to deliver increasingly advanced programs to address the needs of the Java community. Working closely with Sun will help them provide tools to use and develop ever more highly functional applications.

Third parties develop clones of Sun's Java— and intriguing mutations

Cloned Java environments provide an alternative to Sun's original. These clones adhere closely to Sun's specifications for the language and the virtual machine. The added value of the commercial Java implementations lies in their ability to meet specialized objectives, or simply to produce faster executables. Even early Java interpreters developed by third parties improved execution speed by a factor of three or four, and their JIT compilers usually deliver better performance than Sun has achieved.

Others have entirely rewritten the Java environment to optimize it for specific tasks. The Portable Executive for Reliable

Control (PERC) from NewMonics, for instance, is specialized to the needs of embedded systems running applications that require precise timing of control and response, such as multimedia, telecommunications, and robotics. To satisfy these timing constraints, PERC tunes the garbage-collection and thread-handling mechanisms described in Sun's Java execution model; as a result, applications provide smoother and more effective performance. By expanding the scope in which Java is employed, NewMonics and others demonstrate the breadth of its capabilities.

Hardware Devices

Hardware developers will also have a supporting role in Java's future. The introduction of Internet appliances (IAs) adds to the variety of computer systems available to home and business users. These devices aim to make mass access to the Internet easy and inexpensive. Designing them around the Java virtual machine frees manufacturers from any need to develop platform-specific application suites, and thus enables them to concentrate on building the most cost-effective hardware. Java reduces hardware costs still further by eliminating the need for some components: because they download nearly all their software, Internet appliances do not need their own storage devices.

An Internet terminal in every family room?

Some Internet appliances incorporate Java chips, microprocessors that execute bytecode directly. By using Java chips developed by Sun and others, IA manufacturers aim to simplify the architecture of their products, and to achieve better performance than a Java interpreter can provide.

Figure 11.1
Java: interpreted, compiled just in time, and on a chip

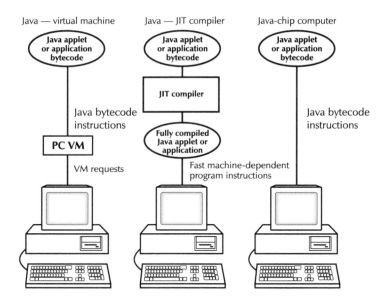

Java returns to its roots

Java chips can bring the functionality of the Java environment to simple, portable electronic devices, as well. Java processors can make such devices smarter, more highly interactive, and more flexible, because they can run programs from the expanding base of Java code. Use of Java in such systems takes it back to its infancy, when it was still named Oak and Sun hoped that it would find success in the consumer-electronics showcase.

Object Technology

Java supplies girders and trusses for the bridges CORBA builds

Object technology is changing the way applications and information interact in today's ever more extensively networked corporate world. Using the CORBA standard and others, an application can obtain useful services from objects running on systems utterly different from its own, and perhaps thousands of miles distant.

While CORBA builds the bridges between applications, Java provides a language to create them. Java is well suited to corporate networks, typically composed of platforms of many kinds. Its object-oriented nature fits well within the object-connection model defined by CORBA. The future will see object technology pervading networks more broadly and more deeply, and Java will be integral in this development.

Technologies that Compete

Java's early acclaim has inspired development of similar products. Microsoft and AT&T's Bell Labs are leading the development of systems often marketed as alternatives to Java. Right behind them are smaller developers, whose products will also concern those interested in Java's future.

Java will have to defend its turf against strong challenges

Microsoft

Perhaps the most determined attempt to confine Java's expansion will be Microsoft's. Sales of Windows 95 and Windows NT are driven by the huge base of applications available for them. The open-systems concept that characterizes Java gives consumers the freedom to abandon these environments in favor of UNIX, OS/2, and others without compromising their range of choices. Microsoft thus has more to lose from Java's success than anyone else in the industry. It is no surprise that the leader in desktop software has devised a comprehensive Internet strategy, intended to establish a strong defensive position, or at least organize a measure of damage control.

Microsoft bases its approach to managing distributed processing across the Internet on the OLE (Object Linking and Embedding) technology it designed as a foundation for application connectivity. "ActiveX technologies" constitute the company's direct answer to Java. ActiveX controls (formerly called OCX controls) are executable components that can be developed in a number of languages, including Java. Designers of Web pages embed applets created with ActiveX controls in much the same way they embed Java applets. "Active scripts," written primarily in Visual Basic Script, serve to glue together components. Microsoft is relying on the famil-

ActiveX is Microsoft's proprietary response to Java's open-systems approach

iarity of these technologies and integration with its popular applications to elicit industry support.

Microsoft licensed Java from Sun early in 1996, and began to incorporate it in ActiveX and other products; in fact, controls created with ActiveX attempt to envelop Java by treating applets as COM (Component Object Model) objects.

ActiveX lacks Java's levels of security and portability

While ActiveX resembles Java in some respects, its dearth of security features and lack of cross-platform support will impede acceptance. Microsoft has tried to patch the security gap by incorporating digital signatures into ActiveX controls to authenticate them. The "trusted" controls and objects this approach yields are only a hollow solution, however, since they still have open access to the computer system once downloaded. Java, in contrast, has language-level features that impose additional security rules on Web-based applets.

Other companies have tried to bring ActiveX controls to non-Windows environments. These do not provide, however, the basic Windows applications framework the controls need to support all their features. As a result, apart from simplified demonstrations ActiveX has not run on non-Windows platforms, and faces serious challenges in gaining the broad industry support Java has received.

Bell Labs

Bell Labs contrives an infernal device to bedevil Java

Bell Labs is also developing a system to compete with Java. Inferno is a networked operating system suitable for a variety of devices and computer platforms. Its cross-architecture design and portability make it suitable for both traditional computers and consumer-electronic devices. The Inferno specification consists of a native programming language (Limbo) and a virtual machine (Dis). The similarities between Inferno and Java are clear and significant.

The Limbo language resembles Java in its garbage collection and multithreading capabilities. Programmers who have difficulty grasping OO concepts find Limbo relatively easy to

CHAPTER 11 • THE FUTURE OF JAVA

learn because its syntax is based on Pascal and C, and because it is not a pure object-oriented language. That lack of "purity" complicates runtime type checking, however, so program execution is not as fast as it might be. Inferno uses reference-count techniques for garbage collection—which surprises experts, who consider reference counting an inferior method.

Like Java, Limbo relies on a virtual machine, called Dis. Programs compile into bytecode that Inferno interprets or recompiles at run time. Dis should outperform most virtual machines because it is modeled on a simple RISC-like register machine, and thus maps easily to the underlying hardware of modern systems, but this advantage is at least partly offset by the runtime type checking Dis requires.

Dis resembles the Java virtual machine, but lacks security features

Instead of building features into the virtual machine to handle security issues, as Sun's model does, the Bell Labs model has Inferno enforce security at the system level. Access to resources available to applications is controlled by management of exclusive namespaces. The namespace constraints are eased for files or remote machines that are authenticated or specified by trusted machines or applications. Although these features are designed around a relatively secure operating system, the developers admit that it does not enforce security rules as strictly as Java does.

Inferno and Java are designed to solve many of the same kinds of problems, and indeed their underlying structures are very much alike. Bell Labs intended Inferno primarily for small interactive devices, rather than for general-purpose systems. This specialization puts it at a disadvantage against Java, which is well suited for both roles, and for others as well. Whether Inferno will capture a significant share of its niche may depend heavily on whether Bell Labs can run fast enough to overtake Sun's lead.

Java is suitable to a wider range of applications

The Crystal Ball

No doubt other competitors will arise to challenge Java in the marketplace. More than one company has risen to fortune by copying and then improving on a successful product: the original IBM PC begat the Compaq; dBase begat Fox; Visicalc begat 1-2-3, which begat.... Given this history, what is to prevent a new product from stealing Java's market?

What features would help a competitor give Java a run for its money?

To defeat an established market leader, a new challenger must offer the customer a recognizable net advantage, come in at a lower price, or both. At this writing Java is free, and it is hard to imagine what package of features would give a challenger an edge over Java's unique combination: object orientation, architecture neutrality, networking support, built-in security, multithreading, synchronization, and simplicity. Even taken by itself, the portability of any Java executable to every popular platform must be seen as powerful discouragement to any potential competitor.

Only Microsoft would seem to have the clout to produce a successful proprietary equivalent to Java—and even its present dominance is not sufficient to guarantee success when its nemesis runs perfectly well on its own flagship products, and on all its competitors' as well.

Java offers more scope for its allies than for its opponents

Innovation and competition in third-party software are more likely to support Java than to oppose it. Developers have ample scope to produce better, faster, more efficient implementations of the Java virtual machine and JIT compilers, integrated development environments and toolsets, applets and applications, class libraries—why take on the unenviable challenge of bucking a widely accepted standard?

It is astonishing that a programming environment so recently out of its infancy should be so well poised to take and hold so dominant a role in the computing industry.

Glossary

abstraction

A process of defining problem solutions in terms further and further removed from their implementation on an actual computer, so as to make it easier to manage program complexity.

API—applications programming interface

A documented list of operations a program can invoke to obtain services from a lower-level system, such as a class library, a GUI, or an operating system.

applet

A small program designed to be distributed across a network (usually the Internet), often to add extra functionality to some other program (usually a Web browser).

application

A computer program designed to perform a specific task.

bandwidth

A measure of the amount of information that can be transferred across a communications link in a specified amount of time. Often measured in bits per second (bps).

bytecode

A compact but portable form of executable instructions. When produced by a Java compiler, bytecode is platform-independent, and is translated to native code when the program is run.

Café

Symantec's Java development system.

cast

To convert a datum from one type to another.

class

A category of objects, or a programmer's definition of such a category. By defining a class, a programmer specifies the shape and behavior of all objects later defined to be instances of that class, including the data they will contain and the operations they will perform.

client

A program which issues commands to a server and uses the data that is returned. A Web browser is an example of a client program.

compiler

A program which translates a computer program from the human-readable (source) form into an executable format, either machine-specific instructions or an intermediate form such as Java bytecode.

debugger

A program designed to help the programmer isolate errors in a program.

Delphi

A RAD (rapid application development) system from Borland.

distributed processing

Sharing subtasks of a large software system among multiple computers on a network.

dynamic linking

The formation of the application from its constituent parts at execution time; differentiated from static linking, i.e., binding components together before distribution.

encapsulation

The process of protecting parts of a program and its data from unwanted access or alteration by other parts.

garbage collection

The process of recovering space that previously held information in the computer's memory but which is now no longer in use. Java uses an automatic garbage-collection mechanism that frees the programmer from a sometimes onerous burden.

host

The computer on which a program is running.

HotJava

Sun Microsystems' own Java-based, Web-browser program.

HTML—Hypertext Markup Language

A simple data format used to create hypertext documents, e.g., Web pages, that are portable from one platform to another.

IDE—integrated development environment

A tightly organized collection of development tools, usually including a text editor, a compiler, a debugger, and resource editors.

inheritance

Using an existing class as the basis for creating a new one. One of the basic mechanisms for developing object-oriented software.

Internet appliance

A low-cost computing device designed to work as an Internet terminal.

interpreter

A program which performs the actions as directed by the source code or intermediate code (e.g., Java bytecode) at run time.

intranet

A private local- or wide-area network based on Internet technologies.

IPC—inter-process communications

Mechanisms by which individual programs can exchange information at run time.

JavaScript

An interpreted scripting language, which despite the name offers very few of the benefits normally associated with Java proper.

JDK—Java Development Kit

Sun Microsystems' collection of programs and resources used to develop programs using the Java language.

JIT compiler—just-in-time compiler

A program which translates bytecode to machine-specific instructions, but does so as a program is loaded.

LAN—local-area network

A group of computers, within a limited geographical area, connected by communications links for the purpose of sharing data and programs.

Latté
The code name for Borland's Java Rapid Application Development System.

link
To join together program components compiled earlier.

native code
The instructions specific to a particular processor, which it can execute directly.

object
A self-contained software entity that contains both data components and the instructions that manipulate them. Objects are often analogs of entities in the real world.

OO—object-oriented, object orientation
A paradigm for software development in which elements of the system are modelled as objects.

P-code
A form of bytecode found in the UCSD-P system of the early 1980s.

platform
The underlying software or hardware on which a program runs. In this book, it refers more precisely to a particular operating system running on a particular computer.

platform-dependent
An adjective describing programs that can run only on a single target platform.

platform-independent
An adjective describing programs that can run on multiple platforms without change.

plug-in

A program designed to add extra functionality to a Web browser. Unlike applets, plug-ins are platform-dependent and must be explicitly downloaded and installed before they can be used.

pointer

A datum which holds the address of another datum, used to refer to that datum indirectly. Software reliability is hard to achieve when programmers are obliged to use pointers rather than more direct means of reference.

polymorphism

Obtaining a service from objects of different but related types as if they were all the same type.

processor

The silicon chip (or chips) at the heart of any computer responsible for executing the instructions contained in a program.

RAD—rapid application development

A system designed to streamline the development of software. Such systems often use highly interactive visual interfaces, and allow systems to be built by combining standard building blocks.

range checking

The process of verifying that a program does not attempt to access information beyond previously specified bounds.

real-time

An adjective used to describe systems whose performance adheres to various rigorous timing constraints.

MAKING SENSE OF JAVA

resource editor

A program that enables software developers to create and modify items such as dialog boxes, menus, icons, and help files.

SDLC—software development life cycle

The series of stages in which a software system is developed and maintained.

server

A computer or program that supplies information to another. Examples are a Web server that supplies HTML documents describing Web pages, and a database server that supplies data requested by a client program.

simulation

A computer program which models a task or process. Perhaps the most familiar example is a flight-simulator program, which allows the user to practice flying skills on a computer.

subclass

A class which inherits features of another class (a superclass) as part of its definition.

superclass

A class whose features have been inherited by subclasses (q.v.).

TCP/IP—Transmission Control Protocol/Internet Protocol

The underlying protocols used to transfer data across the Internet.

thread

A path of execution within a program. A program containing multiple threads can perform multiple operations concurrently.

toolset

A collection of programs and resources for the creation of software. Typically it includes a compiler, a debugger, a resource editor, and documentation.

Trojan Horse

A program which appears to be a bonafide application but which, when run, subverts the integrity of a computer. Named after the Trojan Horse of mythology, which was not what it appeared to be.

virus

A malicious program which damages or destroys the data on a computer system.

VM—virtual machine

Among Java developers, the computer as seen by the Java compiler, as opposed to an actual, specific computer. The compiler produces bytecode for the Java Virtual Machine, which can be translated to processor-specific instructions at run time by an implementation of the VM. Some also refer—confusingly—to that implementation as "the virtual machine."

WAN—wide-area network

A collection of computers located in geographically separate locations and connected together by communications links for the purpose of sharing data and programs.

WWW—World Wide Web

The dispersed, globe-spanning network of HTML "Web" pages.

Index

(Italicized entries refer to margin notes)

C

C 4, 29, 64–65, 70, 78, 80, 82,
    83, 91–101
C++ 4–5, 23, 36–37, 38, 64–65, 70, 78,
    80, 82, 83, 88, 91–101, 110
  backward compatibility 37
  for Windows 128
Café 146
cast 146
class 32, 33, 35, 97, 99–100, 146
  built-in 112
  business-specific 101
  foreign 112
  library 88, 101–102, 105
  loader 111, 112
  local 112
  string 95
client 131
client-server 44–47
  environments 70
COBOL 72
code
  procedural 91, 92–93
  reuse 35–36, 89
  source 39
Common Object Request Broker Architecture
    (CORBA) 71–72
compilation, conditional 93
compiler 39–40, 146
  multi-pass 94
Compuserve 131
concurrency 81
conditional compilation 93
consultants 69
consumer-electronic devices 84–85, 140, 142
continue 95
contract programmers 69
copyright 119
  notice 120–121
CORBA (Common Object Request Broker
    Architecture) 71–72, 140
corporate net 20

D

data
  encapsulating 33
  hiding 32–33
database 71, 76, 113–114
debugger 146
Delphi 102–103, 146
  for Windows 128
developer support 67
digital signature 21
Dimension X 69
Dis 111, 142
distributed processing 56, 141–142, 147
drag-and-drop programming 102–103
Duke 52, 118
dumb terminals 7–12
dynamic
  browsers 45
  linking 103, 147

E

EarthWeb 69
embedded system 85, 139
encapsulating data 33
encapsulation
    25–26, *29*, 29–33, *31*, 40, 88, 147
encryption 21–22, 58–59, 122
error reducing 33
Excel 79
execution speed 77, 83, 138

F

FaxMail 59–62
file servers 13–14
foreign classes 112
FORTRAN 29, 70
freelancers *69*

M

Macintosh 108–109
macros 93
mainframe 7–12
mentoring 105
method 91–92
Microsoft
    59, 73, 79, 125–126, 127, 128, 131, 141–142
minicomputers *10*
Modula-2 96
Mosaic 3
MS-DOS 23
multi-pass compiler 94
multilingual software 98
multiple inheritance 35, 99–101
multiple platforms 89
multiple threads 81–82
multithreading 139
multithreading capabilities 142–143

N

native code 149
net
  corporate 20
Netscape 58, 59, 128
  Navigator 3, 20, 43, 46, 112–113, 131–132
network *71*, 137–138, 140–141
  LAN 13, 13–14, 114
  WAN 19, 114
networking applications 70
NewMonics 139
Novell 128

O

Oak 2
object 32–33, 149
  CORBA-compliant 71–72
  linking and embedding (OLE) 141–142
  management group 71–72
  orientation (OO) 29–38, 140–141, 143
  request broker (ORB) 71–72

object-oriented (OO)
    88–89, 91–93, 93, 103–104, 149
  programming 27–38, 29–38
  programming system (OOPS) 31–32,
    36-37, 69
Objective-C 38
OCX 141–142
ODBC 71
OLE (object linking and embedding) 141–142
operating system 22–24, 38–39, 41, 79
  platform 38–39
  QNX 47–48
operator overloading 94–95
optimization 84, 94, 99
Oracle 128, 132–135
ORB (object request broker) 72
OS/2 23, 125–126, 130, 141

P

P-code 77, 149
Pascal 29, 37, 80, 97, 110, 125
PCs 12–13, 108–109
PERC (Portable Executive for Reliable Control)
  138–139
perceived performance *81*
performance 75–86
personal computers *12*, 12–13
PGP (Pretty Good Privacy) 21
PIMs 70
platform 22–24, 38–39, 40, 41, 47, 49, 149
  independence
    46, 48, 83, 89–90, 93–94, 104
platform-dependent 149
platform-independent 149
plug-in program 45, 49, 150
pointer 96, 99, 150
polymorphism 88, 150
portability *39*, 89–90, 93–94, 104, 142
Portable Executive for Reliable Control (PERC)
  138–139
porting 39
preprocessor 89, 93
Pretty Good Privacy (PGP) 21

V

variables
  global 95–96
  raw pointers 96
variants 34
VDT (video display terminal) 8
verifier 111
version control 103
video 69
video-display terminal (VDT) 8
virtual
  environments 69
  machine (VM)
    40, 41, 46, 72, 75–76, 90, 110–112, 142, 152
  reality modeling language (VRML) 69
viruses 107–109, 152
  Macintosh 108–109
  PCs 108–109
  UNIX 108–109
  Windows 108–109
Visual Basic 64–65, 72, 73, 80
VM (virtual machine)
    72, 75–76, 90, 110–112, 142, 152
VRML (virtual reality modeling language) 69

W

Wall Street Web 57
WAN 114
WAN (wide-area network) 19, 152
Warp 125–126, 130
Web
  browsers 43, 107. *See also* browsers
  page 43, 119
  Runner 2
  server 44
wide-area network (WAN) 19
WIN-OS/2 130
Windows 23, 108–109, 125–126, 130, 141
Windows 3.1 23
Windows 95 23
Word 79
word processing 76
workstations 13–16
WWW (World Wide Web) 152